PARABLE–SEEDS

Second Sowing

Jackson Day

PARABLE–SEEDS

Second Sowing

Jackson Day

ISBN 978-1-64370-173-8

OTHER BOOKS BY JACKSON DAY

The following books by Jackson Day are available to help improve your Bible Storytelling skills:

- **Old Testament Bible Stories** ISBN 978-0-9797324-0-9
- **New Testament Bible Stories** ISBN 978-0-9797324-1-6
- **Bible Storytelling Tools** ISBN 978-0-9797324-2-3
- **Key Bible Stories** ISBN 978-0-9797324-7-8
- **Preaching With Storytelling** ISBN 978-0-9797324-8-5

Other books by author:

- **Story Crafting** ISBN 978-0-9797324-3-0
- **Parable Seeds: First Sowing** ISBN 978-0-9797324-4-7
- **Quick Scripture Reference for Life-Issues** ISBN 978-0-9797324-5-4
- **Outlines of Great Bible Themes** ISBN 978-0-9797324-6-1
- **PRAYER: Not My Will but Your Will** ISBN 978-1-64370-174-5

These books may be order from:

- Amazon.com
- barnes&noble.com
- Jackson Day <biblestorytelling.org>

CONTENTS

FOREWORD

STORY OF TRUTH AND PARABLE

Once upon a time there were twin brothers, Truth and Parable. Both brothers dedicated their lives to the same purpose: to teach people what they should believe and how they should behave.

Truth was in a hurry to teach people, and he left without taking time to clothe himself. Parable was also eager to fulfill his mission to teach, but he took time to clothe himself with stories.

Truth had a lot to say. Truth traveled to different towns and villages. Truth constantly went to the market square to teach everyone what they should believe and how they should behave. However, people simply retreated in disgust at the sight of naked Truth. They turned away, one after another, saying, "Oh, it's naked Truth!", or "Truth is disgusting!", or "Save us from awful Truth!", or similar exclamations.

Truth knocked on many doors, desiring to enter homes and teach inhabitants what they should believe and how they should behave. However, people slammed their doors on Truth. Naked Truth disgusted people everywhere he went. People turned away, fled, and refused to listen to Truth's message. Town after town, Truth walked away in despair; people needed to hear Truth for their own good, but few listened to Truth.

Many years passed. One day, Truth entered a new town, still determined to teach people. Truth arrived at the market square and saw his twin brother, Parable, standing on a platform with crowds listening to him. Parable was dressed in splendid clothes of beautiful stories. The crowd cheered Parable and loved his stories.

Parable finished telling his stories and rushed to greet Truth, his twin brother. Parable asked Truth, "Tell me, brother, what makes you look so sad?"

Truth replied bitterly, "Ah, brother, things are bad. Very bad. I'm very, very old, and no one wants to acknowledge me. No one wants anything to do with me."

Parable answered, "No brother, people don't run away from you because you're old, I'm also very, very old. But the older I get, the more people like me. Listen to my secret; people prefer to hear what they should believe and how they should behave when it's clothed in story. Let me clothe you in splendid stories, and you'll see that the very people who pushed you aside will invite you into their homes and be glad of your company."

Truth took Parable's advice and clothed himself with beautiful stories. And from that time on, Truth and Parable have traveled hand in hand.

JESUS THE PARABLE TELLER AND LOGIC-DRIVEN PAUL

Jesus knew that people receive truth best when it was clothed in story. That is why when Jesus spoke to the crowd, He didn't say anything to them without using parables (Mark 4:34). Jesus mastered the art of clothing truth with stories. Jesus' parables didn't illustrate His message; His stories were His message. Jesus told stories in order to put His listeners on the road to truth. Most of the time, Jesus didn't even explain His parables. At the end of many parables Jesus said, "He who has ears, let him hear."

Story was Jesus' form of speech. Jesus did not come to earth as a theologian; He came as a storyteller. Jesus did not lecture using point-driven abstract language. Jesus told stories every time when He spoke to crowds. Common people gladly heard Jesus tell His parables. Christians who are faithful to Jesus' message need to be faithful to imitate Jesus' storytelling approach.

The apostle Paul spoke and wrote using the philosophical, abstract, logical discourse of the educated. The New Testament had a place for storytelling Jesus and point-driven, logic-driven Paul. Christian academics emphasize point-driven, abstract, and logical interpretation of the Bible and overlook storytelling. Christian academics may suppress storytelling, but will never kill it. Philosophical, logic-driven systems come and go, but great stories keep reappearing. It's like the kudzu vine in the deep South. The farmer may fight it, and think it's gone, but it keeps reappearing and spreading.

The invention of TV started a storytelling paradigm shift. Throughout history, people heard stories from storytellers they knew; such as family members, neighbors, teachers, and religious leaders. TV viewers hear stories from strangers working for global media corporations interested in profit making. Throughout history, storytellers told stories to put listeners on the road to what they should believe and how they should behave. Electronic storytellers aren't concerned about the well-being of their listeners; they only want to make a profit.

Most people hear stories better than they hear truth framed in point-driven abstract logic. Listeners struggle with the meaning of point-driven abstract logic, but they identify with the simplicity of a story. Listeners find point-driven abstract logic boring; however, a well-told story is fun for listeners. Listening to stories can be the most enjoyable and effective way to receive truth.

Whenever and wherever stories are told, a chord is plucked within the understanding of the listeners. Often the story is heard by the ear, but listened to by the subconscious mind where its deeper meaning resides.

I had the joy of living in Brazil for thirty-three years. Storytelling is rooted in the Brazilian culture. I always carried 3"X5" cards in my pocket. Whenever I heard a story I liked, I made notes on a card and threw it into a "story seed box." I collected story books in Portuguese and found story-seeds in many of them. The majority of the stories/parables I tell were adapted from stories I first discovered in Brazil.

I have a strong conviction that before we can change someone's beliefs, we must change the stories they hear and believe. I'm convinced that the shortest road to lead a person to the truth is to tell them a story. Just as Jesus crafted and told stories to put people on the road to truth; I'm crafting and telling stories to put people on the road to truth.

A parable is a fictitious story; however, it is also a true-to-life story that communicates truth. A parable is a fictitious, concise story that illustrates how a person should behave, or what they should believe. It has a moral or religious life-lesson. It is truth clothed in story.

A Christian parable is a fictitious story about ordinary men and women, in familiar settings of life, whose everyday experiences teach divine truth. A Christian parable is not about a giant of the faith; it is about a common person. It's a fictitious story, but it seems entirely probable.

A parable is truth clothed with a story. A parable deals mainly with everyday human life, but its overtone reaches into spiritual life-lessons. A parable contains a subtext that suggests a life-lesson about how people should behave or what they should believe. The subtext life-lesson is usually unspoken, but it is obvious to observant listeners. Parables are straightforward and obvious; they don't teach hidden or secret truths. Each parable has a point that the spiritually observant listener should understand. All listeners hear a good story, while the spiritually observant listener hears a word from God.

Christians should become like Jesus and speak in stories. Jesus told parables to put His listeners on the road to truth. I'm attempting to imitate Jesus by crafting stories that will put listeners on the road to truth.

WHY THE NAME "PARABLE SEEDS"

The title of this book is *PARABLE SEEDS; Second Sowing.* I have already published the book, *PARABLE SEEDS; First Sowing.* I have many seed-ideas for stories, and I constantly discover new ones. I dream of sowing a third, fourth, fifth, and more *PARABLE SEEDS* books.

A seed needs to be planted and watered. It germinates and begins to grow. A tiny seed will grow into a larger plant. Then the gardener hoes around the sprouted plant to remove weeds that would choke it and prevent it from becoming a mature plant. A seed that germinates and matures will produce a harvest of many more seeds.

Each story found in this book contains a seed of what one should believe or how one should behave. When you read or listen to these stories, allow these seeds to be planted in your own life. Take time to water them by thinking and then searching to determine what the Bible says about the life-lesson revealed in the story. You may need to hoe around the sprouting plants by changing some of your thoughts or actions. My desire is that some of these seeds will germinate and grow inside you to produce a bountiful harvest.

Often, the storyteller can't tell if he is getting his message across to listeners. The storyteller is similar to a DJ at a radio station. The DJ's station transmitter is sending out a signal. However, the DJ doesn't know to what frequency the receiver is tuned. In the same way, the storyteller is sending out a story; however, the teller doesn't know to what frequency the listener is tuned.

Jesus told a parable that may help the storyteller deal with this uncertainty. Jesus said, "The Kingdom of God is like this. A man scatters seed on the field. Both during the night when the man is asleep and during the day when he is awake, seed are sprouting and growing. The man doesn't understand how it grows. The soil produces the grain on its own accord– first the stalk, then the head, then the full kernel in the head. As soon as the grain is ripe, the man starts to reap because the harvest has come" (Mark 4:26-29 my paraphrase).

Jesus told the parable to illustrate that the Kingdom of God will achieve its full development by virtue of its own hidden nature. But the parable also illustrates the nature of storytelling. The storyteller who narrates stories to communicate biblical teachings is like the farmer who scatters seeds. Stories have within themselves a life-giving nature capable of sprouting, growing and bearing fruit in listeners' lives. The storyteller can't understand how it happens. A good story begins to grow within the listener when the storyteller ends his tale. The farmer plants seeds every year without knowing if the weather is going to cooperate to make a bountiful crop. In the same way, the storyteller should keep telling stories even though he doesn't know if his listeners will cooperate to help the story grow. The storyteller's primary task is to tell the story. Then, he can trust the story to sprout, grow and produce fruit, even though he may not understand how it will happen.

SUGGESTED WAYS TO USE THESE PARABLE SEEDS

Use Stories to Illustrate Biblical Truths

I became a pastor when I was twenty-six years old. I'm now in my seventies. Whenever I preach or teach, I follow this principle: "Only teach or preach a biblical truth when you have a story to illustrate it." If a teacher or preacher really understands something, no matter how complex it may be, he or she should be able to illustrate it with a story.

Use Stories to Communicate Truths That Are Hard to Swallow

When I was a child, the doctor prescribed for me a bottle of bitter medicine. After the first spoonful, I refused to open my mouth for Mother to give me another spoonful. She promised me cookies; then she threatened a spanking, but I refused to open my mouth for the bitter medicine. Mother mixed the bitter medicine into a glass of orange juice. I drank the medicine mixed with orange juice, but I wouldn't take the medicine by itself. There are biblical truths that are hard to swallow. If the truth is mixed into a story, it is easer to swallow. Often the naked truth is ugly, repulsive, uncomfortable and hurtful. However, when truth is clothed with a story, it becomes more attractive.

Use Stories to Communicate Truths While Entertaining

I retired from Christian ministry when I reached sixty-two years of age. I've recycled myself into becoming a storyteller. I joke to friends, "I tell tall tales on Saturday night and then go to church on Sunday and tell true Bible stories."

Many people will listen to a storyteller but will never listen to a preacher. An organization invited me to do Bible storytelling training in Jacksonville, Florida. My host lived in a large apartment complex and sent invitations to other residents of the complex to come to a Bible study one Wednesday night. Twelve people showed up. Then my host sent invitations to residents to gather on Friday night and hear a storyteller. More than seventy-five people came to the storytelling event!

When I entertain as a storyteller, my goal is that everyone be entertained with some good stories and that those who are spiritually sensitive would hear a word from God. Usually, after a gig, a few people will approach me to talk about one of my life-lesson parable stories. On one occasion a man told me, "When you told that story, I felt God speak to me."

The New Testament values both storytelling-Jesus and philosophical-Paul. Therefore, the Christian church should value both storytelling and the interpretative, logic-driven emphasis. There are people who will never listen to the truth presented in interpretative-logic-driven language, but they will accept the truth when it is clothed in a story.

We need Christians who tell stories that entertain their listeners, while giving a word from God to the spiritually sensitive. We need the casual storyteller telling tales to co-workers at a coffee break, we need the preacher or teacher who illustrates biblical truths with stories, and we need the professional performing storyteller.

Use Stories to Teach in Discussion Groups

I've told many of the stories in this book at church on Sunday nights. I'd tell the story, then I'd ask the following questions to create discussion.

- What life-lesson is illustrated by this story?
- Is the story's life-lesson true to Scripture?
- What scriptural teaching does the story illustrate?
- How should I apply this illustrated life-lesson to my life?
- Do I need to share the insight I received from this story with someone? Who?

I encourage you to try the method.

A DREAM, MURDERED WITH WORDS

Robert was an only child. He was raised on a farm in the deep South, and there were no nearby families with children his age. The child, Robert, dreamed of playing the trumpet in an orchestra. Robert listened to classical, jazz, and country music on the radio, always listening for the trumpets. Robert's father gave him a cheap trumpet on his fifth birthday. Then when Robert was twelve years old, his parents gave him an expensive trumpet for Christmas.

There were no nearby families with children for Robert to play with. So, the trumpet became his best friend. He took his trumpet onto the front porch and imitated the sounds of the wind blowing through the trees. When it rained, he imitated the sound of falling water. He took his trumpet down by the pond and imitated frogs croaking. He walked through the woods and imitated the songs of birds and the noise of squirrels. He walked by the creek and imitated the sound of running water. He took his trumpet to the barn and imitated the sound of horses neighing, cattle mooing, and pigs oinking.

When Robert was sad, his music was soft and slow. When he was happy, his music blasted out. When he was home at night, Robert turned on the radio and listened to classical, jazz, and country music, accompanying the music with his trumpet. Robert's country school didn't have a band teacher; however, Robert took piano lessons and learned to read music. No one taught him to play the trumpet. Robert listened to classical, jazz, and country music on the radio and accompanied it with his trumpet, learning on his own.

Robert was sixteen years old when he heard on the radio that a renowned orchestra was playing in a small city about seventy-five miles from their farm. Robert begged his parents to take him to the theater where the orchestra was playing. Robert's parents argued the price for the tickets would be very expensive; however, they considered it a small price to pay in order to kindle the dreams of their only son. They agreed to take Robert to hear the orchestra.

Robert couldn't wait for the night to come. He got a haircut and put on a suit. He put his trumpet in its case and took it with him into the theater. Robert insisted that his family get to the theater early, so they could have front row seats. As one of the musicians played a trumpet solo, and Robert closed his eyes and dreamed of the day when he would be on stage playing a trumpet solo. At the end of the show, Robert stood applauding while others made their way out of the theater.

Robert left his parents in the theater, made his way backstage, and knocked on the dressing room door of the maestro. Robert heard a foreign accent invite him to enter. Robert asked, "May I have a word with you?"

The maestro answered, "Make it quick!"

Robert said, "I love to play the trumpet. My family, friends, and school teachers say I have talent. But I've never played before anyone who understands music. Would you listen to me play my trumpet and tell me if I have talent?"

The maestro said, "Happens always at end of a presentation. Go ahead, make it quick."

Robert removed his trumpet from its case and played his best music ever. When he finished, Robert asked, "Do I have talent to play in an orchestra someday?"

The maestro answered, "Non!" with his foreign accent.

Robert replied, "But the trumpet has been my best friend since I was five years old."

The maestro said, "Get yourself other friends. Now go, I'm late."

Robert's dreams died. He returned to his parents with a heart and hands as cold as the frozen words of the maestro.

Robert returned home and packed his trumpet case in his closet, never to pick it up again.

Twenty years passed. Robert left the farm when he went to the university and he became known as an outstanding young lawyer. Robert lived in a metropolitan center. One night, Robert and his wife went to a theater to hear an orchestra. To Robert's surprise, the maestro was the same one who had provoked him to desist from his dreams of being a musician.

After the presentation, Robert approached the maestro and said, "I was sixteen years old, you directed a performance in the deep South, and you changed my life. I was a young farm boy who lived to play the trumpet. I insisted you hear me play and you bluntly told me I had no talent."

The maestro grinned and replied in broken English, "That what I tell all who ask my opinion."

Robert said, "You mean that I could have become a great musician?!"

The maestro answered, "Certainly not. If you wanted to be musician, you would not quit when one person say you have no talent."

Robert answered, "But you are a maestro in music!"

The maestro answered, "New talent wants my opinion after every presentation. Let me show you."

Then the maestro called over the young lady who played first chair violin. He asked her, "When you, a teenager, come backstage, played for me, and asked me if you have talent, what I tell you?"

The young lady answered, "You said I had no talent."

The maestro asked, "What you do?"

She replied, "I asked my parents to send me to a music conservatory. I was determined to prove you wrong. I finished my course, auditioned with the orchestra, and I've been here ever since."

Robert was perplexed, but he had learned a great lesson. That night he went home, opened a dusty case and removed his trumpet. It was time to reconnect with an old friend.

Robert realized the power of words. He realized that our words of incentive or discouragement can change another person's life, sometimes for the better, sometimes for the worse. He also realized that our reaction to the words we hear can change our own lives, sometimes for the better, sometimes for the worse. Robert knew that words were the heart of his work as a lawyer, and he determined he would never use words as an instrument to murder someone's dreams. He determined that whenever someone shared their dreams with him, his words would fan the fire of their dreams.

AMERICANS IN SOUTH AFRICA

A delegation of United States prison officials traveled to South Africa to participate in an international conference. The American delegation visited several South African penitentiaries before the conference.

The first prison visited was Pollsmoor Prison in Cape Town. The American delegation was in the warden's office when the warden mentioned, "Americans give me lots of problems."

An American visitor reacted, "You invited us to visit your prison; how we are giving you problems?!"

The South African warden explained, "Oh, I don't mean you. I mean the USA gang in my prison. USA gang members call themselves Americans. They're not American citizens, but they call themselves Americans. It's a gang of the 'Colored.' Coloreds are descendants of White people who settled in African and intermingled with national Africans. USA gang members identify with Black-Americans more than with Black Africans. Most of them have never had a job; they mug and kill to buy food and to feed their drug addictions.

"USA gang members must be high school graduates; they pride themselves as being superior to gangs whose members may not have finished elementary school. A person must shed blood in order to become a USA gang member. Gang members imitate what they see on American TV shows and movies such as *Rambo*, *First Blood*, *Terminator*, and *Godfather*. The gang members shop at clothing stores specializing in outfits with American symbols, like jogging suits that say Yankees, Redskins, or Cowboys. They call their leaders the White House and their fighters the Pentagon."

The United States delegation walked through the Pollsmoor Prison. They saw prisoners with USA tattooed in red, white, and blue on their forearms. One prisoner, with a red, white, and blue USA tattoo asked the delegation, "Hey, are you Americans?"

A warden from the United States answered, “Yes, we’re Americans.”

The prisoner replied, “I’m an American too.”

The United States warden asked, “Were you born in the USA, or were your parents Americans?”

The prisoner answered, “No, I was born in Cape Town. My parents are from Cape Town too, but I belong to the USA gang, so I’m an American!”

The United States warden asked, “Why did you choose the name USA for your gang? Why do you call yourselves Americans?”

The prisoner answered, “Ain’t you an American? You ought to know! You’re rich; you take what you want. Your president is our hero; he takes what he wants. Our gang admires the violence of your country.”

That night, the American delegates sat in their hotel lobby. They pondered and talked about the strange combined impact of poverty and U. S. television on a fragile population. Even from thousands of miles away from the United States, South Africa was influenced by images of Rambo, cowboy movies, gangster movies, and police TV shows. They talked about how the South African USA gang perceives that United States citizens are like the Americans whose stories appear on the daily police news and fictitious films about violent Americans.

ANGRY WHILE IN LOVE

Grady was the vice principal at a middle school and Alice taught sixth grade math. Both were single when the school year started in August, but they got married at the end of the school year in June. The next school year started again in August. Each morning Grady and Alice rode to school in the same car.

The first Friday morning of November, Grady mentioned, “I’ll be glad when Thanksgiving gets here. I look forward to hunting with my father and brother during Thanksgiving break.”

Alice said, “Aren’t we spending Thanksgiving with my family? It’s a family tradition for the women in my family to do our Christmas shopping together on Black Friday.”

Grady replied, “In my family, the men always hunt together during Thanksgiving week.”

The morning conversation started normal, but soon escalated to a place neither one wanted to go. Grady was the first to raise his voice, but Alice responded in kind. They both were shouting and neither one was hearing the other. Their voices grew louder before Grady stormed out of the house and drove away to work, leaving Alice to drive alone. Grady left Alice in a silent house. Alice drove to work in silence. The silence between the two increased as they avoided each other at school. Grady stayed in his office during lunch time in order to avoid seeing Alice in the lunchroom.

Their home was deafeningly silent when both returned from school. Each relived the argument and switched between regretted words spoken in anger and thoughts of more insulting words that could have been spoken. Each feared to be the first to break the silence; each imagined that any spoken words would be misunderstood.

Grady had a headache from the strain. Grady took a book onto the back porch in order to get out of the house; however, he could not focus on his book.

Grady's duties as vice principal required him to be at Friday night football. Grady started out the door and Alice asked, "Aren't you going to eat before the game?"

Grady answered, "I'll grab a bite on the way."

Alice answered, "There's food in the kitchen."

Grady answered, "I want more than a sandwich."

Alice answered, "There's stew in the Crock-Pot that I fixed before I left for school."

Grady asked, "You cooked dinner for me when we were fighting and you were angry at me?"

Alice replied, "I'm angry, but I still love you."

Grady sobbed as he ran to hug Alice.

Grady ate his stew in silence, but before walking out of the house for the football game Grady told Alice, "I'm glad I married you."

ARTIFICIAL FLOWERS

A craftsman's hobby was making artificial flowers. The craftsman created artificial flowers that looked just like flowers grown in a garden. The craftsman went to arts and crafts shows, fairs, flee markets, and market days to sell his artificial flowers. The craftsman was proud that his artificial flowers looked just like real flowers. The craftsman always brought three vases of different kinds of flowers, and he put an artificial flower in each of the vases with the real flowers. The craftsman then attracted customers by offering a prize to passer-byers if they could look at his three vases, without touching the flowers, and discern which one was the artificial flower in each vase.

Many people tried, but no one had ever picked out all three artificial flowers. At one arts and crafts festival, a farmer took up the challenge. The farmer stood about six feet away from the flowers, and he took his time. Then quickly, the farmer pointed out the artificial flower in each vase. The craftsman and all bystanders were astonished and exclaimed, "You didn't even get close enough to examine the flowers! How could you tell which ones were the artificial flowers?"

The farmer answered, "Simple, I watched to see where the bees landed. No bee landed on the artificial flowers. There's no nectar in artificial flowers."

ATTRACTIVE DANGER

Mama Rat and her children lived in a barn. Mama Rat needed to leave home to find food for the family. Mama Rat told her little Rat Children, "I must get us some food to eat. Now, don't leave the den. Don't go out to play. The world outside is attractive, but it's dangerous outside. Sometimes the most attractive things are the most dangerous."

As soon as Mama Rat left, the little Rat Children ran to the door of the den and looked outside. It was a beautiful day. They saw animals in the yard, and they looked like they would be great playmates. Two animals were close to the door of their den. One was sleeping and the other was a big bird with a large red comb on the top of its head. It walked around scratching and clawing at the ground.

The sleeping animal looked so innocent and friendly. It had beautiful soft, silk-like hair. When it breathed, if made a musical purring sound. The Rat Children passed their hands over the soft, silk-like hair. They enjoyed listening to the music of the sleeping animal's purring. The little Rat Children were about to wake the sleeping animal and see if it would play with them. Then, the big bird flapped its wings and crowed a loud "cock-a-doodle-doo." The terrified little Rats ran into their den, and stayed inside until Mama returned.

Mama Rat returned. The Children Rats told Mama Rat about their adventure. "Oh Mama, you're right it's dangerous outside. We found this beautiful animal with soft, silk-like hair that we wanted to play with. When it slept, it made such a peaceful, soft, musical purring sound. Then this monster of a bird terrified us. It flapped its wings and crowed a horrible terrifying sound. Oh, Mama, it scared us!"

Mama Rat said, "I warned you to stay inside because you don't know what's dangerous. The big bird that frightened you with it crowing sound would never hurt you. But the cat that you found so attractive is our greatest danger! Sometimes the most attractive things are the most dangerous."

BATTLE AGAINST ONESELF

Once upon a time, in a faraway land, dangerous giants lived in a big forest. Brave knights lived in a castle within the forest and protected the people of the forest from the dangerous giants.

A magician created silver shields for each of the brave knights. Each time a knight would do a good deed, his silver shield would shine brighter. Each time a knight was brave in battle, his silver shield would shine brighter. However, if a knight were lazy or cowardly, or arrogant, or proud, his shield would become increasingly cloudy, until the knight would be ashamed to bear it. On rare occasions, if a knight showed exceptional courage and devotion to duty, a shiny golden star would appear in the center of his shield.

One day, the dangerous giants gathered to make battle plans to attack the castle and drive the knights from the forest. Spies told the lord of the castle that the dangerous giants were planning to attack the castle. The lord of the castle gathered his knights to attack the giants before they reached the castle.

The youngest knight in the castle was Young Sir Roland. He had only recently acquired his shield and had yet to go into battle. When Young Sir Roland learned that the knights were going to war against the dangerous giants, he dreamed of distinguishing himself in battle, and he dreamed of his silver shield shining brighter. But the lord of the castle ordered Young Sir Roland to stay behind and guard the castle's drawbridge. Young Sir Roland was to prevent anyone from crossing the drawbridge over the moat and entering the castle while the knights were on the battle field.

Young Sir Roland was very disappointed. He felt embarrassed as he stood at the gate while the knights rode off on their horses to the battle ground. However, he stood erect at the gate holding his new silver shield with his left hand and his spear with his right. He stood guard to prevent anyone from crossing the drawbridge over the moat to enter the castle while the other knights were distinguishing themselves in battle.

Eventually a lone knight carrying a cloudy dull shield rode up wearily. The knight claimed he had been wounded in battle. The knight with the cloudy dull shield offered to trade places with Young Sir Roland. He would stand guard at the drawbridge, out of harm's way, and let Young Sir Roland seek glory on the battle ground. Young Sir Roland wanted to leap at the chance, but realized he had orders from the lord of the castle to stay at his post and not allow anyone to cross the drawbridge and enter the castle. Young Sir Roland reluctantly refused and told the knight with the cloudy dull shield, "The lord of the castle ordered me to stand guard and not to allow anyone to cross the drawbridge into the castle. I can't even allow you to cross the drawbridge and enter the castle."

A short time later, an old woman approached the castle, begging for food. The old woman said she had been near the battle, and that the knights were doing poorly. The old woman accused the young knight of being a coward who was afraid to join his companions on the battle ground. Young Sir Roland gave the old woman food, but resisted the temptation to prove to her his bravery. He wanted to be on the battle ground, but he had orders from the lord of the castle to stand guard at the drawbridge to the castle.

Next, an old man in a long cloak appeared across the moat. The old man said he was a magician, and he wanted to help the knights protect the people of the forest. The magician offered to give Young Sir Roland a magic sword that he could use in the battle to save his comrades from destruction. The magician wanted Young Sir Roland to take the magic sword, leave the gate, and join the battle in the forest. Young Sir Roland was so tempted to join the other knights on the battle ground that he moved back across the moat to raise the drawbridge to cut himself off from the strange old man. Suddenly, the magician threw off his cloak, and began to grow. He turned into a great giant, and howled in frustration at Young Sir Roland before turning back to the forest.

Eventually the company of knights rode back, battle weary, but victorious. As they approached the gate, they stopped in wonder. There, shining on Sir Roland's shield, was a shiny golden star. The knights did not understand how someone who had not fought in battle could earn the shiny, golden star. But the lord of the castle knew, and explained that some of the hardest battles a person must fight are not against an armed enemy. The hardest battles a person must fight are the battles against oneself. In disciplining himself to stand guard at the gate when he wanted to be on the battle field, Young Sir Roland had fought the hardest battle of the day.

BEE ATTACK

My wife and I lived in Brazil for thirty-three years. We lived in Brasilia, the capital city of Brazil, for thirteen years. We left Brasilia to retire in the USA in 2003.

The last year we lived in Brasilia, I was sixty-two years old. On one occasion, my wife was traveling, and I was home by myself. One morning, I rode my bicycle from our apartment building to the park where I regularly enjoyed my morning jog. While jogging, I saw an elderly gentleman who appeared to be having a fit. He was screaming while frantically waving his arms, jerking his cap about and slapping himself with it. Upon getting closer, I saw a swam of bees covering him. They had covered his arms, legs, face and neck. I thought, "I can't just stand by and let the bees kill the old man!"

I took off my shirt and started slapping the bees, trying to drive them away. My action made the bees more violent and a multitude left him to attack me. I became scared to death and started spinning around, frantically waving my shirt, trying to drive the bees away. Then, I took off running. I ran toward a group of men screaming, "Help! Help! Help me!" They weren't about to help me; they took off running the other way. After running about fifty yards, the bees finally left me.

I abandoned the old man, ran to find one of the policemen who patrolled the park. I shouted at the officer, "Radio for help! Bees are attacking and killing an old man!" The bees finally left the elderly gentleman. The last time I saw him, the policemen were helping him into a police car and rushing him to a hospital.

I suffered from multiple bee stings and was unable to jog back to my bike. I walked back to my bike. On the way, I heard several people in animated discussion talking about the bees attacking <u>two</u> old men.

I got on my bike and quickly rode to a drug store located on our city block. I asked for medicine for my multiple bee stings. In Brazil, medicine can be purchased from a pharmacist that would normally require a prescription from a doctor in the USA. I had no money with me, but told them I would go to our apartment and bring back money. However, when I got to the apartment, I only had energy to take the medicine and make it to bed. It was six hours later before I was able to get up and walk back to pay the drug store.

I later learned that because I did not understand bees, my attempt to help the elderly gentleman made the bees angry, and I did more harm than good.

My good intentions, combined with my ignorance produced undesirable results for both him and me.

BETTER THAN HOT BISCUITS

It was a Wednesday night prayer meeting at a country church in the deep South. The church had a new pastor, and the new pastor called on a man to pray who had never before prayed in public.

The man began his prayer, "Lord, I hate buttermilk." Everyone was confused and wondered what kind of prayer this was. The man continued, "Lord, I hate to eat butter." Now everyone was totally perplexed with the man's prayer. The man continued, "Lord, I hate plain flour. But after my wife mixes buttermilk, butter, and flour together, and bakes it in a hot oven, I just love hot biscuits. Lord, help us realize that when things get hard, when several things that we hate come up at the same time, when we don't understand what you're doing; Lord, we need to wait and see what you're making of us. After you get through mixing and baking the experiences we hate, you'll make us into something better than hot biscuits. Amen."

BEWARE OF THE DOG

A traveling couple experienced car trouble on a back road. Their car died and would not start up again. A farmer stopped to help and told the couple that a neighbor of his had a garage and could work on any machinery. The farmer said, "He mainly works on farm equipment, but he can fix anything."

The farmer took the couple to the mechanic. They became nervous when they saw a large sign at the entrance to the property that said, "Beware of the Dog." On the door entrance to the garage was another sign, "Beware of the Dog."

The wife stayed in the car, but the nervous husband entered the garage. Then, he saw a large hound dog asleep on the floor. He saw the mechanic who asked him, "How can I help you?"

The traveler asked, "Is this the dog we're to watch out for?"

The mechanic answered, "Yea, before I put the sign up, folks kept tripping over my dog."

BIBLE DIDN'T HELP DOG

Tim is our youngest son. When Tim was three years old, we had a fenced-in yard, and I bought a Doberman Pincher puppy that we named Prince. Our two oldest sons went to school during the day, and Tim played outside with his dog, Prince.

Prince became protective of Tim. We, his parents, could not discipline Tim in the yard. If we raised our voices at Tim, Prince got between Tim and us. If Tim cried, Prince showed his teeth and became aggressive toward us. If children came to play with Tim, we had to lock up Prince. If a playmate chased Tim, Prince attacked the playmate to protect Tim.

A year passed. Tim was four years old, and Prince was one year old. Tim loved to imitate people. Every Sunday when we came home from church, Doris started lunch, and Tim went to my study to get a New Testament. Then, Tim went to the back yard and preached to Prince. Tim imitated the gestures and voice of our pastor. He held the New Testament in his hand just like the pastor held his Bible. Once, a pastor who had suffered polio as a child, preached at our church. The pastor walked with a limp; and that Sunday, Tim limped as he preached to Prince.

One Sunday, Tim observed his oldest brother, Sam, being baptized by immersion at the Baptist church. We returned home and Tim went into the back yard, filled a bucket with water and poured it over Prince. Tim wasn't satisfied with Prince's baptism, so he filled up the bucket again with water, and chased the elusive dog, around the backyard, trying to finish the baptism. After being baptized, if Tim appeared with a bucket, Prince hid.

On Sundays, Doris called Tim to enter the house for Sunday lunch, and sometimes Tim forgot and left his New

Testament in the backyard. Prince chewed up and swallowed each New Testament left in the yard!

Prince heard the Bible preached every Sunday. Prince “fed on” the Bible and “digested” the Bible. Prince was also baptized; however, he constantly grew meaner toward people who were not part of our family. Even with listening to preaching weekly, being baptized, and “feeding on” the Bible, it didn’t change Prince. Prince always had a dog nature.

BLIND LEADING THE BLIND

A blind man lived in the city and walked to work everyday. He crossed a busy intersection to get from his house to work. The blind man had a mental map of how to get from his house to work. He stepped out of his front door, turned left, walked three blocks, turned right, crossed the busy intersection, and he walked forward for a half block to the office building where he worked. Every day he used his long white cane to follow the sidewalk from his house to the busy intersection. He depended on his hearing to inform him when traffic stopped, and when it was safe to cross the intersection. Most days when he stopped at the intersection and faced the direction he wanted to cross, people who knew the blind man would place a hand on his arm and guide him across the intersection.

One rainy day, traffic was heavy; few pedestrians walked the sidewalk; the pounding of the rain drowned out the traffic noise. The blind man reached the intersection, faced the direction he wanted to go, and stood waiting for help to cross the road. Suddenly, the blind man felt a presence near him. Then, the fellow pedestrian put his hand on the blind man's arm, the signal for him to step onto the street. The blind man stepped onto the street and his fellow pedestrian followed. The two pedestrians were greeted with the sound of horns blowing, squealing of breaks, cars crashing and drivers cursing. The blind man stopped terrified and his companion also stopped.

Police arrived on the scene and discovered two blind men standing in the center of the intersection, one holding onto the arm of the other.

BROTHER LIKE THAT

Life had been hard for Willy. Willy's father left home before Willy was born. Willy's mother put in long hours working as a waitress to provide for Willy and his older brother. Willy's older brother protected him and became a high school football hero. Then, Willy's older brother became a college football star.

Willy's older brother signed a contract to play pro-football. The first thing he bought was a house for his mother and brother Willy. The year Willy was a senior in high school, his football-playing brother bought him a new fancy car as a Christmas gift.

Willy drove his fancy new car to town. He came out of a store, and he saw a teenager admiring his fancy new car. Willy looked at the teenager's faded, patched clothes and could see, life had been hard for the teenager.

Willy opened the door to his new car, and the teenager asked, "Man, is this your car?"

Willy replied, "Yea, my brother gave it to me for a Christmas gift."

The teenager asked, "You mean he gave it to you, and it cost you nothing?"

Willy repeated, "Yea, my brother gave it to me for Christmas."

The teenager said, "Wow, I wish..."

Willy thought he knew what the teenager was going to say. He had heard it many times, "Wow, I wish I had a brother like that."

Willy was wrong because the teenager said, "Wow, I wish I could be a brother like that!"

Willy was so amazed at the teenager's answer that Willy asked the teenager, "Wanna go for a ride in my new car?"

The teenager answered, "Wow, man, I'd love to!"

After a short ride, the teenager had a grin on his face and asked Willy, “Man, would you drive down my street?”

Willy smiled to himself. He thought that the teenager wanted to impress his friends and family with the fact that he had a friend with a fancy new car who would give him a ride. However, Willy had, again, misjudged the teenager.

The teenager shouted, “Stop! Wait just a minute.” Then, he ran into his home. Willy heard him slowly returning and saw him pushing a younger brother in a wheel chair.

The teenager pushed his brother to the car, touched it and told him, “That’s the guy I was telling you about. His brother gave him a new car as a Christmas gift. He has a new car, and it didn’t cost him a thing. Someday, I wanna give you a new car. But, it will be different from this. You’ll drive it with just your hands.”

Willy asked the crippled brother, “Wanna go for a ride?” Willy got out of his car and lifted the crippled brother into the passenger seat. The older brother got into the back seat. Willy felt great joy as he gave them a ride around town and out into the country. That was the beginning of a long friendship between Willy and the two brothers.

Willy realized, it’s good to receive gifts. But blessed is the generous person who delights in giving to others. Willy remembered that Christmas celebrated God giving His son to the world. Baby Jesus grew into a man who taught, "It is more blessed to give than to receive" (Acts 20:35 NIV).

BURNT BISCUITS

Times were hard for the Higgins family during the recession. Mr. Higgins lost his construction job. Mrs. Higgins got a job as a waitress at a local café. She put in long hours to earn little money. Mr. Higgins tried to do the cooking, but the children complained because he always burned something. They refused to eat his cooking. Every night, Mrs. Higgins returned home and cooked supper for the family. Mr. Higgins spent his day working on their house, repairing, painting, and fixing it up. He did things that he had put off when he had a job. The house looked better, but they had very little money.

When Mrs. Higgins returned home extremely tired, she would quickly prepare breakfast food for supper. One night, she made breakfast food for supper. She placed a plate of eggs, sausage, and burnt biscuits in front of Mr. Higgins.

The children watched to see their daddy's reaction. When Mr. Higgins had cooked biscuits, he'd burned them, and the children fussed and refused to eat them. Yet, Mr. Higgins reached for the burnt biscuits, smiled at his wife, and asked the children about their day at school. The children watched their daddy smear butter and jelly on all the burnt biscuits. He ate every bite of every burnt biscuit. He passed the eggs and sausage to the children, but he ate every bite of every burnt biscuit.

The children finished eating their breakfast food for supper, took their plates to the kitchen, put scraps into the trash can, and put their plates and utensils into the sink. Mr. Higgins helped his wife clean the table.

The children heard their mother apologize, "Honey, I'm so sorry I burned the biscuits." Mr. Higgins answer, "Honey, I love burnt biscuits. Now you sit down and rest. I'll do the dishes."

Mrs. Higgins went to bed early. The children finished their homework, and Mr. Higgins put them to bed. The little girl asked, "Daddy, do you really like burnt biscuits?"

Mr. Higgins pulled the covers over his daughter and said, "Your mother put in a hard day at the café. She knows you don't like my cooking, so she insists on cooking, even if she's tired. Besides, burnt biscuits never hurt anyone."

The little girl went to sleep thinking, "When I grow up, I wanna marry someone just like Daddy."

CHARITY UMBRELLA

Liz flew into Portland, Oregon for a job interview. Her interview required her to meet with two different people in two separate buildings. It was Liz's first trip to the Northwest. She arrived in Portland under a drizzling rain the day before her interview and spent a night in a hotel. The following morning, the sun was shining with no clouds in sight, so Liz didn't carry a jacket or umbrella with her when she walked to her first interview.

Liz finished her first interview and went to the building's door to walk to her second interview. She noticed that it was drizzling rain outside. Liz spoke out loud to herself, "Oh no, it's raining. I'll look a mess when I get to my job interview."

A man standing next to Liz said, "You're not from Portland."

Liz answered, "No, I'm not from Portland. How did you know?"

The man answered, "If you were, you would have looked at Mount Hood for the weather forecast. Mount Hood never fails to give you an accurate weather forecast."

Liz asked, "How's that?"

The man answered, "If you can see Mount Hood, you know it's going to rain. If you can't see Mount Hood, you know it's raining."

Liz answered, "I'm gonna look a mess when I arrive at my job interview with my hair and clothes soaking wet."

The man said, "Here, take my umbrella."

Liz answered, "Where would I return it? I don't even know your name."

The man answered, "You don't need to know my name. All you need to know is that I follow Jesus who taught in the Sermon on the Mount that when you help someone with a need, don't let your left hand know what your right is doing."

COACH – FATHER

Coach was the head coach of the Wildcats High School football team. The Wildcats had an outstanding football program. Coach had a son named Eric. Coach and his son Eric played ball together from the time the boy could walk. Coach and son Eric watched football together and the coach/father constantly explained what was taking place on the football field. Coach and his son constantly watched football films together. The coach/father taught his son everything he could about football.

Eric started high school. Before Eric went out to play football, his coach/father warned him that at school, he would be his coach and he would not give his son any special treatment. In fact, he would demand more of his son, so no one could say Coach was showing favoritism to his son. Coach/father was true to his word, he showed no favoritism to Eric on the football field; except, to push him harder than the other boys. As a sophomore, Eric was back-up quarterback and had some playing time in all the games. That was the year the Wildcats made it to the finals of the state championship but were beaten by the Bulldogs.

Eric was the starting quarterback during his junior year of high school. The Wildcats again made it to the final game of the state championship against the Bulldogs.

Toward the end of the second quarter, it was third down and one yard to go. Eric kept the ball on a quarterback sneak. At the snap of the ball, a pile of bodies grew too dense to see through, and a crack was heard throughout the stadium: the sound of two helmets crashing together. The impact knocked the helmet off Eric's head. Eric fell to the ground, and a Bulldog player unintentionally stepped on Eric's head. Eric lay still. The most dreaded site in football is to see a player lying motionless on the ground.

Coach followed his rule of showing no favoritism to his own son. Coach shouted, "We've got first down. We've still got the ball. Get him off the field."

Coach gave instructions to the back-up quarterback while doctors attended his son on the field. Paramedics placed Coach's non-responsive son into an ambulance. Eric's mother ran down from the stands and jumped into the ambulance to ride to the hospital with her son. The ambulance sped through the streets and Eric regained consciousness and began perseverating, saying over and over, "I made first down. I made first down. I made first down." Then he lost consciousness again. He regained consciousness, and he kept repeating, "I made first down. I made first down. I made first down."

Doctors and nurses met the ambulance at the hospital door and rushed Eric into the emergency room. Eric's mother saw bleeding where cleats from the football shoe had opened her son's head. She wanted the doctors to stop the bleeding, but the doctors didn't notice the bleeding from the head wound. They were too busy examining his eyes, ears, nose, and torso. They rushed Eric for a CT scan without stopping the bleeding on his scalp.

After the CT scan, the doctors told Eric's mother that her son had suffered depressed skull fractures. The cleats from the football shoe had caused dents in Eric's skull bone. The doctors recommended emergency surgery to elevate the bony pieces and to inspect the brain for evidence of injury.

Eric's mother called a friend at the game and asked the friend to relay a message for her coach/husband to get to the hospital at once. Coach responded, "Tell my wife, 'I've got a football game to coach, I'll get there as soon as the game is over.'"

Coach's team won the championship. Coach quickly celebrated with his team, gave a short interview to the reporters, and then rushed to the hospital.

His wife screamed at her coach/husband, "Why didn't you come? Why didn't you call? I had to make all the decisions by myself!"

Coach answered, "I had a ball game to coach! I've always told my son that on the football field, I'd treat him like any other boy. I'd show him no favoritism."

His wife replied, "Tonight, your son needed his father, and I needed my husband. If you can't be his father and my husband when our son is non-responsive, and I don't know if he is going to live or die; I guarantee you, he'll never play football for you again!"

The school year passed. A year latter, Coach's Wildcat team was again playing the Bulldogs for the state championship game. Again, Coach's son Eric was the starting quarterback; however, Eric was now the starting quarterback for the Bulldogs.

CRACKED POT

Once, there was an elderly water carrier who lived in India. His father and grandfather had also been water carriers. The water carrier had two large pots. Each pot hung on the end of a bamboo pole, which he carried across his neck. Every day, he would take the two pots to a stream of water, fill his two pots, and then take water to the homes in the village. One pot was perfect and was always full of water at the end of the long walk from the stream to the village houses. The other pot had a crack in it, and by the time the carrier reached the village houses it had leaked half its water.

For a full two years, every day the water carrier brought only one and a half pots full of water back to the village. Of course, the perfect pot was proud of its accomplishments and looked down on the inferior cracked pot. The cracked pot was ashamed of its defect and was miserable because it achieved only half of what it had been made to do.

After two years of what it perceived to be a bitter failure, the cracked pot spoke to the water carrier one day by the stream. "I am ashamed of myself; I beg you to forgive me."

The carrier asked, "Why? What are you ashamed of?"

The cracked pot answered, "Water leaks from the crack in my side. I only deliver half my load because water leaks out all the way back to the village. My imperfection causes you to do all of this work, and you get only a half load from me. I'm a failure, I'm a cracked pot."

The water bearer said, "You're not a failure. When we return to the village, look at the sides of the path and tell me what you see."

They went up the hill, and the cracked pot paid attention to everything he saw. He saw beautiful flowers on his side of the path and noticed that the other side of the path was dry and hard, and there was nothing but dry, dead weeds. But at the end of the trail, the cracked pot felt bad because it had again leaked half its load. Again the cracked pot apologized to the carrier, “I’m a failure, half of the water I was carrying leaked out. I make more work for you because of my imperfection.”

The water carrier said to the pot, "Did you notice that there were flowers on your side of our path, but not on the other pot's side? That's because I know what is wrong with you, and I took advantage of it. I planted flower seeds on your side of the path, and every day while we walk back from the stream, you've watered them. For two years I’ve been able to pick beautiful flowers to decorate my friends’ homes. Because you are a cracked pot, everyone in the village can decorate their homes with beautiful flowers.”

From that day on, the cracked pot knew that even though it had something wrong with it, it helped make the world a more beautiful place.

If you are a cracked pot, you are not perfect, but you water someone else’s path so flowers can bloom. We tend to think that our defects cause problems and pain; however, they also help something beautiful grow.

DANCING TURKEYS

During the 1800's and early 1900's traveling medicine men would show up in a town on market day. The medicine men attracted a crowd with a variety of songs, dances, instrumental music, comedy sketches, tall tales, or performing animals. After the crowd gathered for entertainment, the medicine men would pitch the virtues of a particular patent medicine. Medicine men would hawk brews and potions of herbal medicines that were guaranteed to heal when all else had failed. The medicine men often claimed to possess supernatural healing powers, and on the spot would offer herbal brews to cure everything: ulcers, hair loss, back aches, headaches, ingrown toenail; you name the problem, they would brew an herb for a cure.

One medicine man attracted crowds with dancing turkeys. He put turkeys on a stage and began to slowly strum his guitar. The turkeys slowly danced to the tune. A faster tune was played and the turkeys increased their pace and kept in step. The man strummed a faster tune, and the turkeys kept time. Every time the medicine man changed tunes, the turkeys accompanied with their dancing feet. The medicine man ended his show strumming his guitar as fast as he could play and the turkeys kept dancing in rhythm to the fast music.

The medicine man claimed he had supernatural powers to communicate with wildlife, and that his supernatural powers enabled him to teach turkeys to dance. But, I'm going to tell you how he trained his dancing turkeys.

Before hitting the road for his medicine show, the medicine man put the turkeys on a metal plate above a low fire and slowly strummed his guitar. As the plate heated each turkey would lift one foot up. While one foot cooled, the other got hot so the turkey would swap feet. The heat accompanied the rhythm of the music. Warm plate, slow music. The medicine man increased the fire and increased the rhythm of the music. The hotter the metal plate, the faster the turkeys would dance. The music always accompanied the speed that the turkeys were lifting up and putting down their feet.

After the turkeys were trained, they were put on a stage without the metal plate and fire. For the show, there would be no metal plate, but when the music started, the turkeys remembered the pain and instinctively danced to the music. Only the turkeys remembered the fire that provoked them to keep time with the music.

When you see someone dancing through life, and you don't understand the reason why they dance the way they do, it's possible you don't know about the fire someone previously built under them.

DEALING WITH ENEMIES

Mr. Farmer's neighbor constantly criticized him. The neighbor complained about the stink when Mr. Farmer fertilized his pasture with chicken manure. He complained that Mr. Farmer put his fence too close to the property line. He complained that the cow's mooing kept him awake at night. One day, Mr. Farmer was getting a haircut and told his barber about his fussy neighbor. His barber told Mr. Farmer two stories.

Two Austrialian Shepherd dogs worked together herding sheep. The two dogs constantly fought. If one dog had a bone, the other tried to take it away. If the shepherd petted one dog, the other snapped at the one being petted. The two dogs fought for the attention of the same female dog. The two dogs were always fighting. One day a bear came to steal a lamb from the flock. One dog attacked the bear. The other dog said to himself, "If I don't help my enemy now, the bear will kill him, and later attack and kill me." So, he joined his fellow dog in the fight. After the fight the two dogs made peace.

A congressman was a unique politician in Washington. He was considered an honest politician. In his home town, he lived in the three bedroom house he had when he was first elected. His car was seven years old. He refused favors or money from lobbyists. He was concerned for his constituents. He never criticized members of the other party; he was kind and considerate to them.

No one expected the honest politician to have opposition in the coming election. However, a challenger opposed the honest congressman. His opponent launched a vicious mudslinging campaign with vicious attack ads. He accused the honest congressman of corruption, of hidden wealth, and of hidden motives behind his votes. Letters were sent to newspaper editors with unfounded allegations of the congressman's wrongdoing.

Most people believed the accusations to be false. However, everyone waited for the congressman to defend himself and deny the accusations. Colleagues asked the congressman how he was going to counter the rumors. The congressman told this anecdote, "When I was a boy, my daddy had a coon-hunting hound dog. On nights when the moon was full, that coon-hound howled at the moon all night long. But despite all the dog's barking, the moon kept shining. Well, I'm going to keep shining while my opponent makes all kinds of noise."

The barber then advised Mr. Farmer, "You need to discern if you and your neighbor can come together against a common threat like the Australian Shepherds, of if you need to ignore him like the congressman ignored his opponent."

DEPENDS ON HOW THE DROP FALLS

Granny Day and Grandpa Day were baby boomers from the Civil War. They were born within the year their soldier fathers returned from what they called the Great War of Northern Aggression.

Grandpa lived on the farm his grandfather had settled and cleared in the 1830's. After Grandpa got married, he built an addition to the old log cabin his grandfather had built. His grandparents and his parents lived in the old log cabin, and Grandpa and his bride lived in the addition. Grandpa dug a well right behind the back porch of his new addition. That was a big improvement from having to tote water from the spring about 300 yards away. Granny put milk and butter in a bucket and let them down in the well water to keep them cool.

After World War II, electricity came to rural Alabama, and Granny continued to use the bucket in the well to keep her milk cool. She didn't want a refrigerator. Her children bought her a refrigerator, but Granny never put anything in it. She continued to use the bucket in the well. Granny and Grandpa only used electricity for lights at night.

Granny always cooked on a wood burning cast iron stove. After electricity came to rural Alabama, Granny's children offered to buy her an electric stove, so she wouldn't have to build a fire on hot summer days to cook. Granny didn't want no electric stove. She said, "If you give me a 'letric stove, I ain't gonna use it, just like I ain't never used the 'letric frigerator."

But Granny could bake some mighty fine bread in her wood burning stove. She always cooked biscuits for breakfast, cornbread for lunch, and a small loaf of bread for supper. None of the ladies in the family could make bread as fine as Granny's.

One day when Granny was cooking, Cousin Johnnie dropped in on her. Granny said, “Come on in the kitchen, I just started fixing some bread.”

Cousin Johnnie went into the kitchen. She knew that Granny made delicious bread, and she knew that Granny would ask her to stay to eat some. Granny started mixing up flour, butter, buttermilk, and other stuff. Then, Cousin Johnnie noticed that Granny had a runny nose, and there was a drop hanging from the tip of her nose. Cousin Johnnie kept her eyes on that drop at the tip of Granny’s nose. Granny kept working the dough. Sometimes she leaned over her dough as she was mixing, sometimes Granny turned sideways to talk to Cousin Johnnie, sometimes she raised her head and looked out the window to see if Grandpa was coming in from work. Cousin Johnnie kept looking to see if the drop would fall into the bread dough, or onto the table, or onto the floor.

As Granny worked the dough, she invited Cousin Johnnie, “Won’t you stay and have some of bread with us. It’ll be ready before the dog can wag his tail twice.

Cousin Johnnie replied, “Depends on where the drop falls.”

Granny said, “Ain’t no cloud in the sky. It ain’t gonna rain. Just as well stay.”

Cousin Johnnie still answered, “Depends on where the drop falls.”

So after that, in our neck of the woods, if someone was waiting to see what happened before they made up their mind, they would say, “Depends on where the drop falls.”

DIRTY CLOTHES ON THE LINE

During my childhood, all families washed their clothes and hung them on clothes lines to dry. It hasn't been many years since it was the custom for ladies to hang freshly washed clothes on clothes lines for the sun to dry.

A newly married couple moved into a home in town. Shortly after moving into their new home, the new bride looked out the window and told her husband, "Our neighbor is hanging dirty clothes on her line. My mother taught me how to get dirt out of my wash. If I knew our neighbor better, I'd offer to teach her how to get her clothes clean. Look at those dirty spots on her clothes."

A few days later, the neighbor washed another load of clothes and the new bride again looked out the window and commented, "Look at those dirty spots on those clothes on the line. Our neighbor continues to hang dirty clothes to dry."

The new bride continued to look out the window and criticize her neighbor for not knowing how to get her clothes clean.

A month later the new bride was surprised to notice her neighbors' clothes were white and clean. The bride told her husband, "Look, our neighbor has finally learned to get her clothes clean and white. Do you think someone finally taught her how to wash her clothes?"

The husband replied, "Nope, it was me. Yesterday, I washed and cleaned our windows."

DOC FULLER, OFFICE UPSTAIRS

Some of the best farm land in Alabama is called "The Black Belt." It received its name from the fertile black soil that used to produce bumper crops of cotton. There was a time when Cotton was King in the Black Belt. When Cotton was King, a 120-acre farm might have 40 acres of cotton and the farm would support the landowner and four families of share croppers. When Cotton was King, plowing was done with mules. When Cotton was King, nearby towns had cotton mills that transformed cotton into cloth. When Cotton was King, young people stayed on the farm, worked a few acres of cotton, and worked in a nearby cotton mill.

When Cotton was King, filling stations had three bathrooms: one for white women, one for white men, and one for people of color. When Cotton was King, a café had two dining rooms, one for whites and the other for blacks. When Cotton was King, black and white children rode separate yellow buses going to separate schools. When Cotton was King, small-county-seat towns were prosperous and had hospitals. When Cotton was King, small-county-seat town doctors made house calls to the distant farms.

When Cotton was King, one county seat town in the Black Belt had three doctors when a fourth, Young Doc Fuller, returned home to begin practicing medicine. When Young Fuller was in the local school, some years his father worked as a share cropper, other years he worked as a bootlegger; most years he spent time in jail. Classmates ridiculed Young Fuller by calling his father "White Trash." Young Fuller served in the military, went to college on the GI bill, and went to medical school. Now this son of a white trash father returned to his home town as Young Doc Fuller.

Young Doc Fuller rented a garage apartment that had been fixed up for a now deceased mother-in-law. He rented a space above Davis Seed Store for his office and put up a sign by the narrow stairs, “Doc Fuller, Office Upstairs.”

The other three doctors in town had clinics on the street level across from the hospital. Young Doc Fuller was busier than the older doctors; however, he didn’t make as much money. People with money went to the nicer street level clinics across from the hospital. The poor, both black and white folks who couldn’t afford to pay a doctor, climbed the steps to Young Doc Fuller’s office. Young Doc Fuller didn’t try to collect from those who couldn’t pay. He drove his car to distant farms to treat patients who couldn’t pay. It didn’t matter to him if the patients were black or white.

Young Doc Fuller started courting Miss Mary Jane. Miss Mary Jane had ignored Young Fuller when they were in high school together. Miss Mary Jane’s mother considered Miss Mary Jane an unclaimed blessing, because local young men from families with old-money had overlooked Miss Mary Jane when they were choosing their brides-to-be.

Miss Mary Jane came from a family of old-money. Her great-great-grandfather was a pioneer who settled the county and cleared the land. Her great-grandfather increased the size of the farm, and it became a plantation. Then her grandfather increased the size of the plantation. However, Miss Mary Jane’s father loved hunting, fishing, drinking, gambling, and womanizing more than farming. Land was slowly sold off. The old-money family now had no money, but they kept up the appearance of being a family with old-money.

Miss Mary Jane considered that even though Young Doc Fuller was the son of white trash, his becoming a doctor made him a worthy catch. Young Doc Fuller became engaged to Miss Mary Jane. He bought a lot and built a lovely two bedroom, one bath, cottage for his bride-to-be.

Young Doc Fuller was pleased when Miss Mary Jane said she wanted to help at his clinic after they were married. However, Young Doc Fuller would not have been pleased if he had known that Miss Mary Jane intended to filter out poor patients, collect all unpaid bills, and move his clinic to a building on the street level across from the courthouse. Miss Mary Jane figured that in a few short years, she would live in a two-story plantation home.

Young Doc Fuller and Miss Mary Jane scheduled their wedding for 6:00 p.m. on a Saturday. On their wedding day, about noon, a young black man wearing overalls came to Young Doc Fuller's garage apartment and begged him to help his wife who was having difficulty giving birth to their first child. Young Doc Fuller told the young black man that it was his wedding day and asked him to seek help from one of the other doctors. At 3:00 p.m., the young black man returned – other doctors weren't available. The father-to-be had returned home and the midwife told him that if he didn't get a doctor, his wife and baby would die. Young Doc Fuller grabbed his black bag and his wedding clothes and went with the man.

At four o'clock, Young Doc Fuller sent word to Miss Mary Jane that he was helping with a complicated birth and might be late for their wedding. At 5:30, Miss Mary Jane received word that things were beginning to happen, and Young Doc Fuller should make it to the wedding by 7:00. At 8:00 o'clock, Young Doc Fuller showed up for his wedding; two hours late! Miss Mary Jane met him at the steps of the church screaming, "On my wedding day, the most important day of my life, you care more about a black baby than your own bride!"

Doc Fuller explained that he couldn't let a mother and baby die when he had the ability to save them. Miss Mary Jane reacted in anger and called off the wedding.

Ladies from families with old-money told Miss Mary Jane that she had done the right thing. However, those same ladies, whose daughters were unclaimed blessings, invited Young

Doc Fuller to eat lunch with them after church on Sundays. Many chicken dinners were served, but no courting followed. Young Doc Fuller never dated another lady.

Young Doc Fuller moved into the two bedroom, one bath, cottage he had built for Miss Mary Jane. The kitchen was never inaugurated. He ate breakfast, lunch, and supper at Davis Café across the street from the court house. Every morning, Young Doc Fuller walked by the sign, “Doc Fuller, Office Upstairs” and climbed the narrow steps to his office.

Time came when Cotton was dethroned as king. The government adopted a soil bank program where farmers were paid to replant cotton fields with pine trees. A 120-acre farm no longer supported four or five families. It could not even support the landowner. Tractors replaced mules. One man on a tractor could farm more land than ten families could farm with mules. Many share croppers, both black and white went on welfare. Cotton mills closed; young people left the farms for the cities. Stores in county-seat towns were boarded up. County-seat hospitals closed. Older doctors retired; younger doctors moved their practices to larger towns. Doctors no longer made house calls.

The Civil Rights Movement came into being at the same time when Cotton was being dethroned. Segregation was eliminated. While Cotton was being dethroned; black and white children rode the same big yellow school bus going to the same school. Filling stations with three bathrooms were re-labeled, one for women, one for men, and one for employees only. Cafes with two dinning rooms now had one for smokers and the other for non-smokers.

Doc Fuller was soon the only doctor in his county-seat town. Every morning, he walked by the sign, “Doc Fuller, Office Upstairs,” and climbed the narrow steps to his office. The poor, who could not afford to pay, climbed the steps to Doc Fuller’s office. Families with old-money had a choice, climb the stairs to see Doc Fuller, or drive 50 miles to see a doctor in a larger town. Most climbed the stairs to see Doc Fuller.

Time came when Old Doc Fuller no longer climbed the stairs to his office. His kitchen was finally inaugurated. Some of the women folk, both black and white, who owed Old Doc Fuller for his medical services volunteered to cook, clean his house, and sit with him when he needed around-the-clock care.

Old Doc Fuller died; people filled the church for his funeral; there was standing room only. Noticeably absent was Miss Mary Jane, who was still bitter that on her wedding day, Young Doc Fuller cared more about a black baby than his bride.

The old men who gathered at Davis Café every morning for coffee, talked about organizing a fund to erect a monument for Doc Fuller's grave. One day, Mr. Davis, the café owner, told the old men drinking coffee, "No need to worry about a marker for Old Doc Fuller's grave. Done been taken care of. Remember, Doc Fuller missed his wedding to save the life of a black baby. That black baby is a grown man with grandchildren. It bothered him that there was no marker for Doc Fuller's grave. He don't have no money, but he removed the sign giving directions to Doc Fuller's office and put it on a post. The grave marker reads, 'Doc Fuller, Office Upstairs.'"

GREATEST LOVE WAS A DOG

Jennifer Aniston is a woman envied by many because or her beauty, talent, fame, and wealth. Jennifer gained worldwide recognition for portraying Rachel Green on the television sitcom *Friends.* Jennifer has acted in dozens of films, and she is one of the top ten richest women in entertainment; she earns more than five million dollars per movie.

In June 2011, Jennifer got her first tattoo on the inside or her foot to celebrate the greatest love of her life. The tattoo features the name "Norman," the name of her late Welsh Corgi-Terrier mix dog who died in May of 2011, at the age of 15. Jennifer got the tattoo to celebrate the fifteen years she lived together with her dog, Norman.

Jennifer told *Allure Magazine*, in February of 2011, "Really, the most unconditional form of love that you can encounter is with a dog. They're excited the minute you come home, and they show the same amount of excitement every day. They're loyal, and they're always, always faithful."

Jennifer Aniston is one of the most beautiful, talented, and richest women in America, yet, she lost her greatest love when her dog died. Jennifer prefers dogs to men because they make better companions and offer unconditional love. She also lived longer with her dog that she's lived with any husband.

That got me to thinking about reasons that a four-legged friend is a better companion than a woman.

1. A dog loves it when your friends come over, even if you haven't given a notice in advanced, and even if the house is a mess.
2. A dog will always greet you at the door; it doesn't expect you to call when you are running late, and the later you are, the more excited your dog is to see you.

3. A dog will forgive you for admiring other beautiful dogs.
4. A dog is happy when you leave lots of things on the floor.
5. A dog doesn't mind if you leave the toilet seat up.
6. A dog would rather go for a walk than to go shopping.
7. A dog never expects gifts of flowers, cards, or jewelry for birthdays and anniversaries.
8. A dog is not upset if you forget birthdays or anniversaries.
9. A dog would rather eat a hamburger than eat out in a fancy restaurant.
10. You never have to wait for a dog; a dog is ready to go 24 hours a day.
11. A dog makes a great running partner; it stays by your side and is always ready to go for a run.

I've experienced the love of some great dogs, but the greatest love I've experienced was from people. I've never experienced wealth; however, I've experienced the wealth of loyal friends who have been faithful to me. When I was a child, I loved my Beagle Hounds, but my greatest love was for my parents. When I was in my twenties, I loved another Beagle Hound, but my greatest love was for my new bride. When I was in my forties, I loved my Doberman Pincher, but my greatest love was for my wife and three sons. When I retired in my sixties, I loved my chocolate Labrador Retriever, but my greatest love was for my family–my wife, my sons, my daughters-in-laws, and my grandchildren. I've experienced the love of some great dogs, but the greatest love I've experienced was with my wife who lived with me for more than 52 years.

Jennifer Aniston is a woman envied by many because or her beauty, talent, fame, and wealth; but I pity her if the greatest love she has experienced was from a dog.

DOGS ACTING LIKE CHRISTIANS

Bill had a chainlink fence to keep his Labrador Retriever inside his yard. One day, Bill heard his dog barking furiously. Bill looked outside and noticed another dog calmly standing in the street in front of his house. It interested Bill that his dog inside the fence barked at the dog outside the fence, but the dog outside didn't pay his dog any attention. That is the way it is with dogs.

Bill looked closer at the dog in front of his house. He recognized the dog. It belonged to a family he had visited and invited to his church. The dog must have gotten out of its owner's yard. Bill called the dog, opened the gate and invited the dog into his yard. Bill's Lab stopped barking. The two dogs circled each other, did their sniffing and then proceeded to ignore each other. That is the way it is with dogs; when they are together they often ignore each other. Bill approached the visiting dog and petted it. Bill's Lab quickly ran up to him, raised his leg and marked Bill as his territory. Bill's dog was jealous when his master gave another dog special attention. That's the way it is with dogs.

Bill called the dog's owner to inform him he had his dog. Then Bill realized he had never visited the man or invited the man to his home after the family started attending his church. It occurred to Bill that church members sometimes act like dogs.

The ones inside the church bark at those on the outside, while those outside seldom bark back. However, if an outsider enters the church, after initial introduction, old timers often ignore the newcomer unless they happen to be in their social crowd. If the newcomer receives special blessings and attention from God, old timers feel jealous and want to keep God's special blessings for themselves. That's the way it is with dogs; it shouldn't be the way it is with Christians.

EATEN FROM THE INSIDE OUT

Two marine creatures, a particular type of jellyfish named the Medusa, and a snail named the Nudibranch, are found in the Bay of Naples, Italy. They lead a most unusual life.

Nudibranch snails are different from other snails because they don't have shells and are often called the naked sea snail. The colorful snails are called the "butterflies of the sea." Jellyfish might be attracted to those snails because of their beautiful color. The Medusa jellyfish are typified as free-swimming marine animals consisting of a gelatinous umbrella-shaped bell and trailing tentacles.

The two marine creatures are both found in the Bay of Naples. A mature Medusa jellyfish tangles a newly-hatched snail in its tentacles, believing that it killed the snail. Then, the mature jellyfish engulfs the tiny newly-hatched snail that's just starting its life cycle. The Medusa jellyfish thinks it's getting a tasty meal; however, the Nudibranch snail is not digested by the Medusa jellyfish. Once the snail is inside the jellyfish, the snail attaches itself to the jellyfish's insides and begins having dinner. The snail starts to eat from the inside the Medusa jellyfish, devouring the jellyfish bit by bit, first some part of the inside of the jellyfish, then the tentacles and finally trimming its outer body. The jellyfish is reduced to a small round appendage, affixed to the skin near the snail's mouth. All the time the Nudibranch snail is growing in size, while the Medusa jellyfish is being reduced in size.

FAITH AND ACTION

An adventurous explorer set out to hike across a Brazilian rain forest. The explorer hiked over jungle trails and came upon a large river that he couldn't hike across, neither could he swim across. The explorer followed a trail beside the river, until he arrived at a small village. The explorer asked if there were boats that carried passengers across the river. Someone pointed him toward an old bearded man sitting in front of a hut. The old bearded man offered to take the explorer across the river for a fee. The two men agreed on the fee.

The explorer expected a motorized barge to cross the large river; instead, he was shocked when the old man pointed out an aged canoe carved out of a tree trunk. The explorer and the old bearded man entered the canoe, and water came within two inches of the top side of the canoe. The old man picked up two paddles; each paddle had a word carved onto its surface. One paddle read "Faith" and the other paddle read "Action".

The canoe had only traveled a short distance from the shore and the nervous explorer couldn't contain his curiosity. The explorer asked the old bearded man, "Why are the two words 'Faith' and 'Action' carved into the paddles?"

The old man didn't answer, but he placed the paddle marked "Action" onto the floor of the canoe and he paddled with all his might the paddle marked "Faith." The canoe turned in a tight circle. Then the old man laid the paddle marked "Faith" onto the floor of the canoe, picked up the paddle marked "Action", and paddled with all his might. The canoe turned the opposite direction in a tight circle. Then the old bearded man picked up both paddles and paddled with both of them at the same time. The canoe went forward toward the opposite side of the river.

Only then did the old bearded man speak. “Now we’re headed toward our destination. You saw, it’s necessary for Faith and Action to work together. If you only use one of those attitudes you’ll go around in circles. The same is true for all goals you want to reach in life. You must use both Faith and Action.”

FIRE LESSON

Many years ago, houses in the deep South were heated by wood burning stoves or fireplaces. Often, the kitchen and only one other room in the house would be heated.

During that time, an opinionated church member quit going to church. Several families with small children had joined the church. The church voted to build Sunday School classrooms for the children. It was necessary to cut down a hundred-year-old pecan tree in order to add Sunday School rooms to the church building.

The opinionated church member argued, "My granddaddy planted that tree. When I was a child, the church put tables under the pecan tree's shade, and we had dinner-on-the-ground at homecoming. I don't have anything to remind me of my granddaddy except that old pecan tree."

After the men cut the old pecan tree, the opinionated church member stopped going to church. He stopped talking to the neighbors who went to church.

Weeks passed before the church's pastor visited the opinionated church member. That night, the cold north wind was blowing. The church member knew the reason for his pastor's visit. The church member's voice was as cold as the cold north wind when he told his pastor, "Too cold to stand by the door." Without inviting the pastor to enter his house, the church member turned his back on his pastor and moved to the room with the fireplace. The pastor followed the church member without saying a word. The pastor sat in one rocking chair by the fireplace, and the church member in another. The church member didn't say anything else to the pastor, and the pastor didn't say anything to the man. The two men sat in silence and without moving, watching oak logs burning and dancing fire flames.

After a few minutes, the pastor went to the fireplace and studied the burning oak logs. Then the pastor picked up the tongs used for placing logs onto the fire. He grabbed a bright burning log and placed it to the side of the fireplace, away from other burning logs. Then the pastor returned to his rocking chair and sat without moving or speaking, watching the dancing flames in the fireplace. The opinionated church member still sat without speaking or moving. The two watched as the flames decreased in the lone burning log. Then sparks flew from the lone log and its fire died suddenly. The lone log smoldered and gave off a little smoke. Then the smoke died away. The lone log laid at the side of the fireplace charred and black. No words had been spoken since the opinionated church member spoke with a voice that was as cold as the cold north wind, "Too cold to stand by the door."

After a few minutes the pastor again grabbed the tongs and place the lone charcoaled log on top of the burning logs. At once it again caught fire, giving off light and heat together with the other logs. Flames danced around it and from it.

The pastor stood up to leave and walked to the door without speaking a word.

The opinionated church member spoke, "Thanks for the beautiful sermon. I'll be back in church next Sunday."

Neither of the men felt the cold north wind when the opinionated church member opened the door for his pastor to leave.

FIVE-YEAR-OLD MALIBU

My wife and I were thirty years old when we moved to Brazil to work as missionaries. We raised our three sons in Brazil and stayed in Brazil for thirty-three years.

We knew we would have made more money if we had remained in the States. We were aware that family members with two incomes made much more than we did, but our financial needs were met. We loved Brazil. We loved Brazilians and experienced their love for us. We had the joy of feeling like we were doing what we were born to do. We usually remained in Brazil for four years, returned to the USA for state-side assignment for one year, and then returned to Brazil for four more years.

One year, we were preparing to return to the USA for our state-side assignment. It was the year that our oldest son was going to complete high school and remain in the states for his university studies.

A pastor from Orlando, Florida, visited Brazil and he was a guest in our home. I translated for him when he spoke in Brazilian churches. I mentioned that one problem missionaries have when they go on state-side assignment is buying a car as soon as they arrive. And when one needs to buy a car in a hurry, it's hard to get a good deal.

Two weeks before our state-side assignment, the Orlando pastor called us from the states and said a man from his church had bought five cars auctioned off by Disney World. One car was a five-year-old, low mileage Malibu station wagon. The church member would sell the car to us for the price he paid for it. I didn't remember what a Malibu looked like, but I told the pastor we'd buy it.

We landed in Orlando and picked up the car. A couple of weeks after arriving in the states, we visited my wife's family in Texas. Since we had been in Brazil for four years, it was the first time we had seen them in four years. Her parents, two brothers, and sister all lived close to the Dallas-Fort Worth area.

My wife's family gathered at my in-laws home the day after we arrived in Texas. Several family members were already in my in-laws home when my sister-in-law arrived, excited that she had bought a brand new Cadillac. All the family members rushed to the drive way to look at the new Cadillac that was parked behind our five-year-old Malibu. I noticed that my wife's nieces and nephews, who were still in high school, were driving newer and more expensive cars than our five-year-old Malibu.

Later that evening, I shared with the family how God had blessed us by enabling us to buy the five-year-old Malibu at wholesale price as soon as we arrived in the states. But then I realized that no one in the family understood why we considered it a blessing to be able to buy a five-year-old Malibu.

FREEDOM AT LAST

Once upon a time, in a far away country, a man made his king angry. The king ordered his soldiers to imprison the man in a dungeon beneath the castle. The king turned the prisoner over to a seven-foot-tall, three-hundred-pound muscular jailer who was covered with battle scars. The jailer had a long key attached to his belt, and he escorted the prisoner down a dark stairway. The jailer opened a creaking, groaning cell door and thrust the prisoner into a dark, dusty, and damp cell. The jailer shut the door with a bang, and left the prisoner alone in the dark, dusty, and damp dungeon.

The prisoner remained alone in his dark, dusty, and damp dungeon for ten years. Each day the jailer returned, opened the creaking, groaning dungeon door, and gave the prisoner a pitcher of water, a loaf of bread, and a bowl of soup.

Every day the prisoner felt more abandoned and depressed. After ten years, the prisoner decided that he couldn't stand it any longer. He wanted to die, but he didn't want to commit suicide. The prisoner decided to find a loose stone to attack the giant jailer. The jailer would be forced to defend himself and would kill him. Death would free him from his dark, dusty, and damp dungeon; his misery would be over.

The prisoner made the preparation for his attack. He examined, closely, his dark, dusty, and damp dungeon. He tested the security of every stone in the wall, but couldn't find a loose stone. He then examined the door carefully, hoping to find a loose piece of metal he could use as a weapon. The prisoner caught the door handle and turned it. The door creaked, and groaned, but opened to his amazement. He investigated and found that there was no lock, and never had been.

The prisoner groped along the corridor and felt his way up the dark stairway. Two soldiers were standing by an open door at the top of the stairs. They allowed the prisoner to pass. No one tried to stop him when he crossed the courtyard of the palace. Armed guards standing at attention by the drawbridge allowed the ex-prisoner to leave the walled city and walk away a free man.

Then the ex-prisoner realized that the only thing that kept him in his dark, dusty, and damp dungeon was his false belief that the door was locked. Ten long years, his false belief had imprisoned him in a dark, dusty, and damp dungeon. Any time during the ten years, he could have opened the door he wrongly though was locked, and been freed. The ex-prisoner went home to his family and lived as a free man ever after.

FRONT YARD, BACK YARD

A first year high school football coach described to me his abusive father. The coach compared his father to the yards at their home. The front yard was always manicured with cut grass and beautiful flower beds. Whereas, the back yard had piles of building material, left over from when the house was built. No grass had been planted in the back yard; it was covered with weeds that were mowed about twice a year. In the same way, his father was a gentle, patient, polite, caring man when he was at his store, in town, and at church; however, when he was at home, with just the family, he was sarcastic, cynical, critical, abusive, and impatient.

Years later, at a Writers Conference, a participant asked, “Should one write about true experiences that he believes would help others; however, the facts would create severe controversy in one’s own community and family?”

A discussion followed with no conclusion reached.

I happened to be in the bathroom alone with the writer who had raised the question. I brought the subject up again with him.

The writer confessed that he and his brother grew up in a home with a father who was a hero to many, but he was abusive to his own children. The boys knew that ducking to avoid their father’s fist or sidestepping to avoid a kick would result in a severe whipping. Often, the boys got a whipping and never knew why. They went to school sick because they were afraid their father would whip them for getting sick. If the teacher called their parents to come get them because they were sick, they got a whipping for not telling their parent they were sick. If one son did something wrong, both got a whipping. The father insisted that the family spend Sundays together. Every Sunday the family went to church. Then, they would eat at home, a lunch prepared by their mother. The boys couldn't leave home on Sundays to play with friends. The TV remained off on Sunday afternoons. Every Sunday, something happened that angered their father, and he used his fist, feet, or belt on his two sons. Sunday was the most dreaded day of the week for the two boys.

The father is now dead, and no one outside of the family knows that he was abusive. The town considers the father a hero; he was the local boy who did well and put the town on the map. A park in town is named after him. Every year a high school graduate is awarded a scholarship that carries his father's name. The town is grateful for the generosity of his father that built a community center. Each church in town remembers the generosity of his father in helping with every building project. Public speakers and local pastors often tell stories about the virtues of his father.

The writer feels that people who were raised in abusive homes could benefit from his writing about the struggles he and his brother faced. However, if he wrote about the abusive side of his father, he would destroy the concept the community has of him.

The writer remembers how his mother protected her husband's reputation. On occasions when her husband was drunk and missed appointments, she lied and said that he was sick. When one of her husband's punches or kicks broke one of the children's bones, his mother told the doctor that the boys had been fighting. Once, when her husband hit her with his fist and broke her nose, she claimed that one of her sons had thrown a baseball that hit her in the face. The writer believes that if he were to write the truth about his father, his own mother would call him a liar.

A good question for parents, which is more important: to keep up the front yard, the image the public has of you; or the back yard, the image your children have of you?

GOING WITH THE FLOW

For several years, our family lived in the city of Salvador, Brazil, located on the Atlantic Ocean. Our sons were seven, twelve, and fourteen when we bought three kayaks. We went kayaking in nearby rivers, bays, and the Atlantic Ocean.

Vacation time came, and our family rented a cabin on a river about three miles from where the river encounters the Atlantic Ocean. One afternoon, I went kayaking with my two older sons, Sam and John. We went down river to the mouth of the river where it encountered with the ocean. Near the encounter, we hit turbulent rough waves. The flow of the river encountered incoming waves. Flowing fresh water from the river encountered resistant salt water for the ocean. The encounter of the river with the ocean became our encounter with danger. My son John shouted, “We’re in trouble, we’re over our heads!”

I shouted back, “Head for shore!”

I was in front of my sons. I turned toward the shore, but a wave hit my kayak and turned me around facing the ocean. Every time I aimed for shore, a wave turned me toward the ocean, and the flow of the river moved me closer to gigantic waves. I saw the boys get back into their kayaks to help me and I shouted, “Stay! Stay! Stay!” I knew if they tried to help me, they would endanger their own lives.

The flow of the river took me to encounter a gigantic wave which flipped my kayak. I came out of my kayak. The flow of the river thrust the kayak over gigantic waves into the Atlantic ocean. The river current shoved me close to an island on the opposite side of the river from my sons. Swimming frantically, I made it to the island. I was so exhausted, I laid down on the sand to rest.

We had two kayaks and three people. I was on an island in the middle of the river; about fifty yards from my sons. The river current was too strong for me to swim to the boy's side. I didn't know what to do. The tide began going out and that accelerated the flow of the river. After about an hour, I shouted across the river for the boys to check the beach to see if the wind had blown my kayak to shore. It had, but my paddle was lost. The boys tied a rope to one of their kayaks and to mine, dragged all three kayaks overland a couple of hundred yards from the encounter with the ocean. Then they paddled over to a point on the island where I was located. My sons picked me up and towed me upriver, back to our cabin.

The next day, I returned to the city to buy another paddle. That next night, my son John and I went fishing. We took our kayaks to within a couple hundred yards of where the river encountered the ocean. We docked on the river shore, walked to the ocean and fished until after midnight.

After midnight, we got into our kayaks to paddle upriver to our cabin. We paddled a short distance when a panic attack hit me. I didn't experience panic the previous day when a gigantic wave flipped my kayak; however, that night I was terrified. I was sweating cold drops of fear. I couldn't paddle straight, I went round and round in a circle. I was terrified. I forced myself to breathe deeply and finally gained enough control to straighten my kayak and followed my son, John, back to our cabin upriver.

I told my wife, Doris, about my panic attack. The next morning, she insisted we go to a calm beach. She realized, if I didn't return to a kayak immediately, I never would.

A couple of days later, I jogged on a dirt road by the side of the river to its encounter with the ocean. The tide was coming in. The incoming tide pushed ocean water up-river. I realized that if we had been at the encounter of the river with the ocean when the tide was coming in, the tide would have taken me to safety, away from danger.

I meditated and realized, “Sometimes, the person who goes with the flow will experience the tidal flow carrying him away from danger toward safety; however, the tide always changes direction and eventually will take the person who goes with the flow to encounters with danger.”

GOOD INTENTIONS

The future looked bright for Taylor. In tenth grade, Taylor was a starting running back on his high school football team. His high school coach said, "I've never coached a more talented and disciplined player."

Taylor dreamed of playing football at a university and in the pros.

In eleventh grade, Taylor broke all records made by previous high school running backs in his state. Several university coaches contacted Taylor. In the last game of the season, Taylor was returning a punt when he was tackled hard and suffered a spinal injury. He lost the use of his legs and returned to school in a wheelchair.

The first day Taylor went to physical therapy, his therapist asked him, "What goals do you want to achieve?"

Taylor answered, "I want to walk across the stage to receive my high school diploma."

The therapist replied, "It's a reachable goal, but it will require you to work hard and endure great pain. We got a year and a half to make it happen."

Taylor went to physical therapy three days a week. The therapist started each session by manipulating Taylor's muscles and joints to increase his flexibility, strength, and endurance. Taylor cried out in pain, but he thought, "I'm enduring this pain so I can walk across stage to get my diploma." Every time he fell, Taylor thought, "I'm getting up and trying again, so I can walk across stage to get my diploma." Taylor dreamed of walking across stage to get his diploma the same way he once dreamed of making touchdowns on the football field.

A year and a half passed.

On the morning of May 23, the day of his graduation, Principal Buffet made the decision that Taylor would not walk across the stage to receive his diploma, but Principal Buffet would step down from the stage and hand Taylor his diploma. Principal Buffet told Taylor, "You don't need to struggle to stand up, remain seated, and I'll hand you your diploma."

Taylor argued, "I've pushed myself for a year and a half in therapy, so I can walk across the stage and get my diploma."

Principal Buffet replied, "It's not going to happen. I'm doing this out of concern for your own safety and emotional needs. If you fell in front of two thousand people, you'd be humiliated, and it would destroy you emotionally." Principal Buffet didn't realize that Taylor would be destroyed emotionally if he didn't even try to walk across the stage.

Taylor argued, "If I can't walk, I won't show up for graduation!"

Principal Buffet answered, "It's not going to happen. You're not going to walk."

Fellow students found Taylor sobbing in the bathroom. Taylor told them about Principal Buffet's decision and Taylor's decision not to go to graduation. The students told Taylor, "You better be here tonight. You're gonna walk!"

That night, it was time for graduating students to walk into the auditorium. Students refused to walk on command. They told the supervising teacher, "We want to be treated like Taylor. If Taylor walks across the stage, we walk across the stage; if Taylor remains seated and Principal Buffet brings his diploma to him, we remain seated and Principal Buffet brings our diplomas to us."

The teacher rushed to the stage to tell the principal the students' demand. Principal Buffet snorted, "It's not going to happen. Tell them to start walking!"

The impasse began. Students refused to walk; Principal Buffet refused to agree that Taylor could walk across the stage. After a forty-five minute impasse, Principal Buffet gave in and agreed that Taylor could walk across stage to receive his diploma.

Taylor's name was called. Two football players carried Taylor up the steps to the stage. Then they handed Taylor his walker. It took Taylor a long minute using his walker to reach a red-faced Principal Buffet. However, everyone in the auditorium was standing and cheering. The cheer made Taylor feel better than any cheer he received on the football field.

Taylor is now an attorney who specializes in preventing discrimination against people with deficiencies, and he helps physically impaired people to obtain legal rights.

GREYHOUND RACERS

Shadow, Prince, Princess, and Sport were greyhound dogs who graduated from Kennel School to the race track. They were among the few from Kennel School who made it to the fast race track. Most of their fellow classmates weren't motivated to keep chasing the elusive metal rabbit. They dropped out of school and were never heard from again.

Shortly after arriving at the track, Pepper, the oldest running dog at the track warned the newly arrived dogs, "The fast lane ain't no picnic. Don't think that just because you've arrived at the fast track, you've got it made. You got to stay fast. All my classmates who arrived with me slowed down, dropped out, and disappeared. Run fast or the company will dispose of you. The fast lane ain't no picnic. Every dog is replaceable."

After their first race, the dogs gathered for a conference. Shadow shouted to Prince, "If you hadn't bumped into me, I'd a caught the rabbit."

Prince retaliated, "If you'd got out of my may, I'd a caught that rabbit!"

Princess asked Pepper, "When was the last time you caught the rabbit?"

Pepper replied, "Many a time I almost caught him. But he was always just inches out of my reach. Last week Spot almost caught him, gave it everything he had. He was within an inch of the rabbit when he had a cardiac arrest. Each race, it's getting harder for me to get close to the rabbit."

Shadow said, "If we learn to run smarter, then we can catch the rabbit."

Pepper said, "Big Boss Man is coming, time to get back to our cubicles." The cubicle was what the dogs called their cages.

The dogs started toward their cubicles; however, Big Boss Man stopped Pepper and said, "Old man, you've slowed down," and Big Boss Man took Pepper to the outside door, away from the cubicles, and the younger dogs never saw Pepper again.

After every race the dogs talked about how close they got to the rabbit. They argued and accused some dog of getting in their way. Each blamed another dog for keeping him from catching the elusive rabbit. They talked about how to run smarter; each declared that one day he was going to catch the elusive rabbit.

People who watched the races laughed about stupid dogs who chased the motorized rabbit around the track. People felt superior to dumb dogs who chased a motorized rabbit programmed to stay inches in front of the fastest dog. The stupid dogs were chasing a motorized rabbit they could never catch. However, let us listen to the conversation taking place in one of the viewer boxes at the race track.

"I'd a got promoted if it weren't for George; he took credit for work I've done!"

Another said, "I should have made president of the company; those stupid directors chose a college graduate. I've got the experience; he's only got book learning."

Another said, "I got to get that promotion. Then I can buy a house in a better school district so my kids can get into an elite university. Then they'll become doctors or lawyers."

A coach said, "We'd a made it to the playoff if my quarterback hadn't got hurt. I've got five winning seasons, and after one losing year, they fired me."

A real estate developer complained. "I bought beach property for $800,000. A year later I sold it for a million. Then six months later the guy who bought it sold it for two million. If I'd just held on to that property, I'd a made all that money."

Someone asked Big Boss, "Where's Fred; hadn't seen him lately."

Big Boss replied, "Had to let Fred go."

Someone asked, "Wasn't Fred your top salesman for twelve years running."

Big Boss said, "Yea, Fred was The Big Dog, but he slowed down, started asking for time off to take his wife to chemo. Everybody is replaceable."

HANDICAP ADVANTAGE

Two frogs were hop, hop, hopping side by side. Together, they jumped side by side. They croaked as they jumped and didn't always look ahead to where they were jumping. So they jumped into an open well.

Other frogs saw their accident and gathered around the mouth of the well. Both frogs in the bottom of the well tried to climb out, jumping from one indent in the side of the well to the other.

The frogs at the top of the well shouted, "Don't try to climb out. The sides are too steep, there aren't enough indents in the wall to climb out. You'll kill yourselves trying to climb out."

One frog gave up and swam around and around in the bottom of the well. The other frog continued jumping and climbing. The shouts of warning seemed to inspire him to try harder. Several times he slipped and almost fell back to the bottom of the well. The frogs at the top of the well kept shouting, "Give up, it's impossible, you'll kill yourself!"

The louder the frogs shouted, the more the one frog forced himself to climb out of the well. Finally the frog made it out of the well.

The frogs were saying, "He did the impossible. He climbed out of the well."

Another frog replied, "Didn't do no good to warn him, he's deaf."

HEAVY POTATOES

A seminary trains people for Christian ministry. A seminary professor once told each of his students to bring a large clear plastic bag to class. The teacher brought a large sack of potatoes.

The professor told each student to take a potato for each person who had wronged them that they had not forgiven. He told the students to write the name of the person and the year the person had wronged them. He told them to put the potatoes it in their plastic bag. Some bags were quite heavy. The professor told each student to carry his bag with him everywhere for one week, putting it beside his bed at night, on the car seat when driving, and next to his desk at work.

The hassle of lugging their sack of potatoes around made it clear what a weight the students were carrying spiritually. Each had to pay attention to the sack all the time, so he would not forget and leave it in an embarrassing place. The condition of the potatoes deteriorated to a nasty smelly slime.

The sack of potatoes is a great metaphor for the price we pay for holding grudges against people who have wronged us. Often, we think of forgiveness as a gift to the other person, but it is also a gift to ourselves!

HELP THAT HARMS

Billy lived with his parents in town on a two-acre lot. Billy's father grew up on a farm and loved animals. Billy's father raised rabbits and chickens in the back yard. Billy had chores to feed the rabbits and chickens, and to gather eggs from the chickens.

The hens laid their eggs and walked away. One day, one hen laid an egg and kept sitting on it. Billy told his father, "One hen won't give me her egg. She won't leave her nest. She keeps sitting on her egg."

Billy's father answered, "She's gone broody. She wants to start a family."

Billy's father said, "Billy, I need you to help me make the hen a cozy nest for her to sit on her eggs. We'll make a broody box similar to a small doghouse. We'll make it 15 inches square and 16 inches tall. It'll have a roof with an opening in the front, so she can come and go at will. We'll put some hay inside for her to sit on."

Billy helped his father make the broody box, and he watched his father move the hen and her eggs to the new box. Billy's father explained that the hen would keep the eggs at the perfect temperature to incubate them.

Every afternoon, Billy returned home from school and ran to the hen's broody box to see if the chicks had arrived. The hen became cranky and pecked at Billy when he got too close. She never left the nest for more than a few minutes at a time to eat, drink, and stretch. She puffed herself up and clucked when she was off the nest. Billy tried to shoo her away from her broody box so he could get a better look at the eggs, but the hen made it clear that she wasn't going anywhere. For 21 days, Billy kept checking on the hen and her eggs.

On the twenty-second day, Billy checked on the hen, and he saw several yellow chicks huddled under the mother hen; however, two eggs were not fully hatched. Billy saw the little bodies pulsing and struggling for freedom through tiny holes pecked out of the shells. Billy decided to help the struggling chicks. He took one of the eggs, gently pulled the shell open, and peeled the shell away to free the chick.

As soon as Billy helped the baby chick out of its egg shell, the baby chick gasped, struggled and stopped breathing. Billy took the baby chick in his hand and ran to his mother for help. He told his mother how he helped the baby chick.

Billy's mother said, "Billy, I know you meant to help the baby chick. But each chick has to struggle to free itself from its egg. It must struggle to become strong enough to live outside its shell.

"Billy, sometimes your parents, and others who love you, want to help you in the same way as you tried to help the little chick. But, some things in life we just can't do for you. You have to struggle to do them yourself. If we help you avoid struggles, you won't be strong enough to live on your own. Sometimes when we help someone avoid struggles, we harm them instead of helping them."

HER FAULT

My wife and I were eating at the Fried Green Tomato Restaurant in Montgomery, Alabama. Six inches separated our table from the table next to us, where two men were sitting.

My wife claimed I needed a hearing aid; however, I could easily hear the two men's conversation because one man projected angry words that could be heard halfway across the room. The angry man looked to be in his 60's; his shoulder length hair and beard were obviously died jet black. He wore clothes typically worn by muscle builders, tight-fitting pants and a tight-fitting shirt. But he lacked the muscles. His tight-fitting clothes revealed his protruding stomach. He had the "done-lapped" problem. His stomach done-lapped over his belt. My first impression was, "It's ridiculous the way this old man is trying to look like a young man."

The angry man exclaimed, "My wife Janice got me in trouble with my family. I'm a good man, I've provided well for Janice. I've lived for my wife, children, and grandchildren. I've been a good husband, a good father, and I've been a good grandfather. I have season tickets to my grandchildren's ball games. I've taken care of my family, and I deserve their respect. It's important to me that my children and grandchildren respect me. Janice destroyed their respect for me.

"Janice doesn't take care of her appearance. She's fat. She won't even go for a walk with me. Sometimes when I take her out to eat, she starts arguing with me in the car, and when we get to the restaurant, she refuses to get out of the car and go inside the restaurant. She stays in the car while I go in and eat by myself. In 44 years of marriage; except our honeymoon, we've never gone on a single vacation together.

"I'm entitled to my dream vacation. I'm entitled to do something for myself once in my life. I've been discreet with Kara for three years. Nobody knew. I was careful to protect my family. I decided for once in my life, I'm entitled to a vacation. Kara and I went to the beach. I told my wife Janice that I was on a business trip.

"Janice found my company computer, and she got suspicious. Janice went through my company computer and found e-mails from Kara. On my first night of my dream vacation, Janice called and demanded I return home. I didn't even have one night with Kara. I drove straight home and found Janice lying on the living room floor in a fetal position. And she had called the children and told them about Kara. Now my children and grandchildren are mad at me. If Janice had just kept her mouth shut, I'd still have the respect of my children and grandchildren."

HUSBAND ACCEPTS WIFE

Bill and Sara had been married for two years. They had no children. Both had jobs they enjoyed. Bill and Sara's love for each other kept growing every day.

Sara's company offered a self-help course for its employees, and the facilitator asked each participant to write out 10 goals for self-improvement.

Sara came up with a list of four things she wanted to improve about herself. She asked Bill to suggest six areas where she needed improvement.

Bill refused. Sara went to bed angry, and she refused to let Bill cuddle next to her. She got up the next morning and didn't give Bill his good-morning kiss. Sara and Bill always ate breakfast together; however, Sara left for work without eating breakfast because she didn't want to sit across the table from Bill who refused to give her suggestions on how she could improve.

Sarah's co-workers arrived at work and the other ladies showed their lists for self-improvement; and each mentioned suggestions their husband had given them. Their lists included the following:

- Lose 35 pounds
- Improve on cooking
- Do aerobic exercise
- Go fishing with husband
- Cook supper for the family instead of buying something on the way home
- Organize the boxes stacked in the garage
- Make up the beds every morning before going to work
- Throw away things that weren't being used instead of hoarding things forever

Sara saw the suggestions other men had given their wives for self-improvement. This provoked Sara to feel jealous for her lady co-workers and feel more anger at Bill.

At ten o-clock in the morning, a florist delivered six roses to Sara with the note, “I married you because I loved the person you are. I didn’t marry you to change you. I will help you change to become the person you want to be; however, I will not try to change you. Love, your husband Bill.”

After that, the wives who had received suggestions from their husbands for self-improvement were all jealous of Sara.

ooo

I crafted this story as a Christmas gift to my wife, and I wrote her a note, "To my wife Doris:

"I married you because I loved the person you were as a young lady. I did not marry you to change you; however, you have changed. You are no longer the same woman I married. I love you for the woman, wife, teacher, mother, mother-in-law, and grandmother you have become.

"I also love you because you accepted me and have not tried to change me; except, you tell me how to drive, you try to get me to put the toilet seat down, and to pick up after myself. You have helped me to change in order to become the man I desired to be and to achieve my dreams.

"I am confident that we will continue to love each other as we continue to change in the years ahead.

"Merry Christmas, I love you."

ICU-FILM

I was forty-nine years old, and my wife, my three sons, and I were living in the city of Salvador, Brazil. I got sick. At the beginning of my sickness, my symptoms were so general that doctors couldn't discover my problem. I experienced fatigue, flu-like symptoms, tiredness, muscle pains, and joint aches. Some days I experienced a low-grade fever; I suffered occasional headaches, loss of appetite, nausea, and abdominal discomfort. I experienced discomfort but was able to continue most of my normal activities.

Different lab tests and x-rays didn't reveal the cause of my discomfort. Doctors said my symptoms were generalized and didn't point toward any one specific illness.

One evening our family was preparing to go to a friend's home for a meal. I suddenly doubled over with severe cramps on my left side and broke out with a cold sweat. My son John ran to a neighbor, who was a doctor, and begged him to come at once. The doctor checked my blood pressure, and it was very high. He saw that my pain was on the left side, and I was covered with a cold sweat. The doctor told my wife, "Get him to the cardiac hospital immediately."

My wife was a cautious driver who often provoked other drivers to anger by never, ever going over the speed limit. But that night, race drivers would have envied the way my wife wove in and out of traffic as she raced me to the cardiac hospital.

After initial exams, doctors weren't sure if I had heart problems or something else. I was a jogger who, on most mornings, jogged six miles before breakfast. I was unaware that joggers sometimes have unusually slow heart rates. My normal resting heart rate is in the high 30's or low 40's. The doctors didn't ask, and I didn't mention the fact that I was a jogger.

The doctors put me in the Intensive Care Unit. I was wired to different machines. Every time my heart rate went to the low 50's alarms went off and nurses rushed to my side. I was visited by several doctors. I observed their concern and asked why I was receiving so much attention. Nurses tried to calm my fear by telling me that patients in ICU receive close monitoring.

After observing that when a certain alarm sounded, nurses rushed to my side, and different doctors were called in, I realized, "I'm in ICU. People who are at risk of dying are put in ICU. When that alarm goes off, nurses and doctors rush to my side. It's possible I could die and meet my God tonight."

The thought hit me that if I died, God could show me something similar to a film of my life. Then the thought hit me; what if after God showed me a film of my life, He showed me another film of what I could have accomplished with my life. If there was a deviation between what I had accomplished and what I could have accomplished, I'd be disappointed.

I spent two nights in ICU. On the third day, a doctor noticed that the whites of my eyes were yellow. He suspected hepatitis, released me from ICU and sent me to doctor who specialized in hepatitis. And I did have hepatitis.

After my experience in ICU, I have tried to live my life so that if, after I die, God were to show me a film of my life and another film of what I could have accomplished, there would not be much difference between the two films.

IMITATOR

A club promoted an amateur talent night every Friday. One Friday night, a comic entertained the audience with imitations of different animal sounds. His final performance was of a pig squealing. The audience loudly laughed and applauded. A young man shouted, "That ain't no squeal of a pig!" It was obvious to everyone the critical guy was uneducated. He spoke like a red neck country hick.

The emcee challenged the country hick, "You think you can do better, then show us a pig squealing!"

The country hick responded, "Next Friday night, I'll show you how a pig squeals."

The audience laughed, doubting the country hick could do anything near as good as the comic.

Next Friday night the young country hick returned to give his imitation of a pig squealing. The comic went first, did his imitation of a pig squealing, and the audience loudly applauded. The country hick got on stage, bowed his head, and squealed. The audience laughed at his hideous squealing and booed him.

The emcee asked the audience, "Who did the best imitation of a pig squealing?" The emcee pointed toward the comic, and the audience clapped and whistled. The emcee pointed toward the country hick and the audience booed. The emcee proclaimed, "The winner of the pig squealing is the comic!"

The country hick opened his coat, pulled out a pig and shouted, "You think you're smart; look what you've been booing!" He pinched one of the pig's ear, and the pig let out a hideously loud squeal.

INSENSITIVE TO SURROUNDINGS

My family once lived in a log cabin by a mountain river, twelve miles south of Pagosa Springs, Colorado. Our property bordered the San Juan National forest. A mountain rose from the back of our property. We lived in a valley that was 7,000 feet above sea level, but we were surrounded by mountains that reached above 12,000 feet. A few peaks topped 14,000.

Pagosa Springs is one of the most beautiful places on earth, truly a paradise to live in and a paradise to visit. Pagosa is surrounded by the largest contiguous wilderness area in the U.S.A. Pagosa Springs is an amazing place to live, visit, or explore!

One spring morning, I was jogging on the highway that paralleled a mountain river. A caravan of motorcycles passed me. The bikers and bike mommas looked to be middle aged. One bike mama caught my attention. She was riding the motorcycle's passenger seat, behind a man, and she was reading a book. The woman was insensitive to the mountain beauty; her eyes were glued to a book! The woman kept her eyes glued to a book and missed seeing the snow covered mountain, the mountain river, the wilderness forest, deer gazing in a meadow, and the panoramic view from the top of the mountain pass.

ooo

I attended a conference where a famous man was a keynote speaker. People crowded around to chat with the famous man after every session. People sought to eat at the famous man's table and visit with him. One noon meal, the famous man came to the table where I was eating lunch, looked at an empty chair and asked, "Is this chair taken?" We were thrilled to share the table with this famous man. A college student, who was employed to sell books at a display table, was eating at our table and seated next to the empty chair where the famous man sat down. The student was wearing earphones, listening to music from his i-pod. Professors, attending the conference, envied the student's opportunity to converse with this famous man; however, the student was unaware of his opportunity. The student was insensitive to the presence of the famous man because he focused on listening to his i-pod.

IT'S A MOCKINGBIRD

The sixty-year-old daughter visited her eighty-four-year old mother who had fallen. The daughter came to help for a couple of weeks while the mother recovered from the fall and regained her strength so that she could walk around without a walker.

The two were in the living room. The mother was sitting in her granny rocking chair, reading a book, while the daughter reclined in a La-Z-Boy recliner, reading a book on her iPad.

Suddenly, a slender bodied, gray bird landed on the windowsill behind the mother and belted out an endless string of more than ten different bird sounds.

The mother asked, "What was that?"

The daughter answered, "That was a Mockingbird, mimicking the songs of several different birds."

After a couple of minutes of silence, again the bird loudly and in rapid succession belted out the sounds of different birds.

The mother asked, "What was that?"

The daughter replied, "Mother, I just told you; it's a Mockingbird."

Meanwhile the Mockingbird was conspicuous as it ran and hopped along the windowsill. It again made its presence known to the two ladies inside the room by belting out an endless string of several different bird sounds.

The mother asked, "What was that?"

The daughter raised her voice, "Mother, it's a Mockingbird! It's a Mockingbird!"

After a couple of minutes of silence, the Mockingbird belted out another endless string of several different bird sounds.

The mother asked, "What was that?"

The daughter screamed with irritation, "Mother, I've told you a dozen times; 'It's a Mockingbird!' Can't you remember? It's a Mockingbird! It's a Mockingbird!"

The mother grabbed her walker, pulled herself up, and made her way to her bedroom. The mother returned to the living room with several old diaries. The mother started keeping diaries when she was a teenager. After a half hour of looking through different diaries, the mother handed one opened diary to her daughter and said, "Read this."

The daughter read the following words in her mother's old diary, "Today was the first warm spring day after a bitter cold winter. Birds returned to our yard after a winter of absence. My three year old daughter napped, and I sat in my rocking chair in front of a window to read. I'd only read a few pages when my little girl came into the room and interrupted my reading by climbing onto my lap. She cuddled against me and laid still; so I continued my reading.

"Suddenly a slender bodied, gray Mockingbird landed on the windowsill behind me. The Mockingbird belted out an endless string of several different bird sounds.

"My daughter asked, "Mommy, what was that?'

"I answered, 'That was a Mockingbird, mimicking the songs of several different birds.'

"My daughter again nested against my breast and the Mockingbird belted out another string of several different bird sounds. My daughter sat up so fast that she knocked my book to the floor. She asked, 'What was that?'

"I again answered, 'It's a Mockingbird, mimicking the songs of several different birds.'

"At first I was irritated that my daughter kept asking me, 'What was that?' Then I realized that this was a precious moment as I held her in my arms and she cuddled against me. We kept sitting and I counted; she asked me sixteen different times, 'What was that?' And each time I answered, 'It's a Mockingbird, mimicking the songs of several different birds.'"

JOINING WITHOUT PARTICIPATING

A pastor greeted visitors at his church one Sunday. A visiting family informed the pastor they just moved into the community and were looking for a church home. The pastor scheduled a visit to their home on Tuesday evening.

The pastor complimented them on how they had fixed up their home. They shared with the pastor where they had moved from, why they moved to the community, where the parents were working, and where the children were going to school.

The pastor complimented the family on seeking a church home as soon as they arrived in the new community.

The father explained that he and his wife had been very active in their former church. They had taught a couples Sunday School class together. The wife sang in the choir, was the substitute pianist, and they were sponsors in their church's youth program. The father was a deacon and on the board of trustees. But the father explained, they didn't want responsibility in their new church. They wanted a church home, but wanted to make trips to the beach or mountains on many weekends. They would be in church when in town, but they didn't want responsibility that would require them to be in church most Sundays.

The pastor commended the family for wanting a church home, but frankly told them that he had higher expectations for people who joined his church. But the pastor wrote the name and directions to a church that would meet their expectations.

The next Sunday, the family drove to the church's address that the pastor gave them. The family discovered an abandoned church where the grass needed mowing and the windows were boarded up. There was a "For Sale" sign in the front yard. The abandoned church showed them the logical consequences of their own apathetic attitude.

JUDGING CHARACTER

Dave and Sue studied at the same university and started dating. Dave told Sue anecdotes about his parent's toy poodle named Princess.

Dave left home for college, and his parents felt lonely in their empty nest. They filled the empty nest with the toy poodle, Princess. Dave accused his parents of going overboard in spoiling Princess. Princess refused to sleep in her doggy bed on the floor; rather, she jumped up on the bed and slept between Dave's parents. Dave's parents considered themselves the poodle's parents, calling, "Princess, come to Mama and Daddy."

Dave disliked Princess but tolerated the dog for his parents' sake. Princess constantly barked at Dave with her high-pitch bark. Dave felt Princess was jealous when his parents talked to him. His parents claimed Dave wasn't home enough for Princess to become accustomed to him.

Dave's parents bought Princess a dog stroller. Each morning, they took Princess for a walk, but Princess had to stay in her stroller. Princess was only allowed on the lawn to do her toilet duty. Then Princess had to return to ride in her doggy stroller. Dave's mother started a blog, writing in the first person as though Princess were talking. Dave showed Sue one of his mother's daily blogs, "Hello, my name is Princess. Look at the picture of Mama taking me for a walk in my doggy stroller. Today Mama took me for a walk in the park in my doggy stroller. Mama cut the walk short because big dogs wanted to play with me. I wanted to play with the big dogs, but Mama wouldn't let me. Mama knows best, she knew the big dogs would get me dirty, or even give me fleas."

Dave's parents took Princess to Puppy School. Princess was the star of Puppy School. But Princess didn't obey commands when she returned home. Princess got attention and treats whether she obeyed the command, “sit,” or if she ran around the room. Princess trained Dave’s parents to obey her commands. Princess had an anxiety problem, she had to sniff the feet of anyone who came to their house. Even if the guest didn’t like dogs, Princess had an anxiety attack and barked in her high pitch until the guest finally allowed her to smell their shoes.

Dave invited Sue to visit his parents’ home to meet his parents, eat lunch, and spend the afternoon. Sue was nervous about meeting Dave’s parents for the first time. Sue cooked herself a breakfast of bacon and eggs before she bathed and dressed. Sue wanted to look her best. She looked at herself in a full-length mirror and noticed that her black shoes were dusty. Sue picked up the paper towel she used to blot her breakfast bacon and used it to clean her shoes. Sue noticed that the bacon grease on the towel gave her shoes a shine, so she rubbed the paper towel all over her shoes.

Dave picked Sue up and drove to his parents home. Sue arrived at Dave’s home, and met his parents. Dave’s mother introduced Princess to Sue, but warned Sue, “It takes time for Princess to warm up to strangers.”

However, Princess smelled bacon grease on Sue’s shoes. Princess followed Sue around and stayed by Sue’s shoes when they ate the noon day meal. Dave’s mother kept saying, “Princess usually doesn’t like strangers, but she really loves you.” Princess followed Sue around all afternoon. Princess ignored Dave’s parents. Sue couldn’t get away from Princess.

Sue and Dave were in the car ready to leave and Dave’s mother said, “Honey, Princess really loves you. Princess is an excellent judge of character. We would be delighted to welcome you into our family.”

JUST A DONKEY

Jack was a young colt donkey. Jack followed his mother and daddy when they carried supplies to different farmer's markets. Sometimes, Jack's owner would ride Jack's daddy, and Jack's mother would carry vegetables to the market. Jack dreamed of the day when he would be big enough to carry loads of vegetables or to give someone a ride.

One Sunday morning, Jack's mother carried a load of vegetables to a village close to Jerusalem. Jack followed his mother. Jack liked to wander off and play, so his owner put a halter on Jack and tied him to a post close to his mother. Then his owner sat on a nearby porch to visit with other men.

Jack observed two men approaching. One of the men spoke to his owner, "The master wants to borrow your colt donkey. He'll send him back."

The men untied the rope that restrained Jack to the post. They started to pull Jack away from his mother. Jack brayed, "Mama, I want my mama!"

Jack's mother said, "Jack, calm down. This is the day you've dreamed about. Today you get to work like your mother and daddy."

Jack brayed all the way to the top of the hill, "Mama, I want my mama!" The two men complained, "I wish this donkey would shut up."

One man pulled Jack while the other walked behind poking him with a stick. Finally they got Jack to the top of the hill. Men removed their coats and made a saddle for a man to ride. The man sat on Jack. Someone started leading Jack down the hill toward the city of Jerusalem. People threw their coats and palm branches on the road. Crowds cheered and screamed, "Hosanna! Hosanna! Blessed is he who comes in the name of the Lord."

That night, Jack returned to the stable and described the excitement of his triumphant entrance into Jerusalem, "People cheered me. They shouted 'Hosanna.' They placed coats on the road to soften the road for me to walk over. They put palm branches to soften the road for me, and they waved palm branches. Did I mention how they cheered me?"

All week long Jack reminisced about crowds cheering and throwing coats and palm branches over the road as he made his triumphant entrance into Jerusalem. The following Sunday, Jack slipped out of the stable. He made his way back up to the top of the hill and started marching down the hill into Jerusalem.

Jack returned home with tears in his eyes. He cried to his mother, "Today, nobody cheered, nobody noticed me. Some people were mean. They called me a stupid donkey and hit me with sticks and said, 'Get out of the way you stupid donkey!' Some people added a second word to my name, and it's not a nice word. What happened mama?"

Jack's mother replied, "Son, without Jesus, you're just a donkey."

LEAVING MY WIFE

The year my wife and I went on medicare, we realized old age was creeping up on us. That winter, we started dreading the yard work for the coming summer. So we decided to buy a motor home, sell the house and travel. One week in February, we bought the motor home. The following Friday, we put the house up for sale, and the next day, on Saturday the house sold. We put our furniture into storage and hit the road. We bought a Jeep Liberty to tow behind the motor home. We made a few short trips to parks in Alabama and Georgia. But in May we headed west, and spent four terrific months in Montana. In September, we left the high mountain country of Montana and headed for Orlando, Florida. We were in Orlando from September through March. We suffered several cold spells where we would have to turn on the heat in the morning before taking a bath. In March, it started getting hot in Florida, and we headed toward cooler Tennessee.

About fifty miles from Orlando, we got on I-75. I stopped at the first rest stop on I-75. My wife stayed inside our motor home. I could have used the restroom in our motor home; however, I like to get out to stretch my muscles. Also, every time we stop, I always walk around the motor home to check that everything is as it should be, and I examined the tow hookup for the Jeep, to made sure everything was working properly.

When traveling, some women spend the entire trip worrying that they forgot to turn off the iron at home or left the stove on. When traveling in the motor home and towing our Jeep Liberty, my wife worried that I forgot to turn the ignition key to the position that allows the steering wheel to turn as the Jeep follows the motor home.

After I had used the restroom, I returned to the motor home and checked all around the motor home, and I checked the Jeep we were towing.

I got into the driver's seat and was ready to take off. My wife said, "I don't remember observing if the Jeep's steering wheel was turning when we first took off. I'm gonna check it."

I had just checked everything on the Jeep. I told my wife, "It's all right!"

My wife only heard, "All right." She got out of the passenger's seat, and left the motor home.

I knew she had left her seat, but thought she had gone to the back of the RV to get something out of the refrigerator, or to make sure the bedroom door or bathroom door was closed. I cranked up the motor home, slowly drove around an eighteen wheeler and headed out to I-75.

My wife observed that the steering wheel was turning properly in the Jeep. Then she waited for me to stop so she could return to the RV. Then she observed me enter the freeway and increase speed.

After driving about fifteen minutes, I began to wonder what was taking my wife so long. I started shouting, "Doris! Doris! Doris." I started looking for a place to pull over so I could check on my wife. Then the thought hit me, "Did she get out to check the Jeep after I told her everything was all right?"

I was looking for a place to pull over when I saw a Florida Highway Patrol car behind me with flashing lights. I pulled over. The officer pulled up beside the motor home. When I stepped out, he asked, "Are you Mr. Day?"

I answered, "Yes, I am."

The officer asked, "Are you missing your wife?"

I answered, "I might be."

Meanwhile, my wife had left her cell phone in the motor home, so she couldn't call me. She didn't know what to do. She saw a Florida Highway Patrol car at the rest stop. Doris knocked on its window and told the lady officer, "I've got a problem. My husband just left me here."

The officer asked, "Did he do it intentionally?"

Doris answered, "No, he couldn't get along without me."

The lady Highway Patrol radioed to the Highway Patrol officer who pulled me over.

The lady officer told my wife, "Get into the car. I'll take you to your husband."

My wife started to get into the back seat. The lady officer said, "No, get into the front seat."

My wife replied, "This is a first for me. I've never ridden in the front seat of a police car."

The Highway Patrol officer with me told me that another officer was bringing my wife. He stayed with me to make sure I didn't leave her again. There have been few times that I have been afraid of my wife. But I was filled with fear as I waited for my wife to show up. When she got out of the highway patrol car laughing, I was relieved. The lady officer's last words to my wife were, "Make him pay for it."

LET THE RABBIT RUN

Different families of ducks, eagles, owls, squirrels, and rabbits lived in the meadow. A creek ran through the meadow, and fish swam in the creek. The grown up animals decided they wanted to have a school, so their children could become as smart as people who went to school.

Some of the grown up animals had traveled to distant meadows and gained knowledge beyond those who had never left their home meadow. The animals with travel experience prepared a curriculum they believed would make a well-rounded animal: running, swimming, tree climbing, jumping, and flying.

On the first day of school, Little Rabbit combed his hair, washed his ears, and he went hop, hop, hopping off to school. His first class was a running class. The students were told to run to the top of the hill and back again as fast as they could go. Little Rabbit outran Duck, Squirrel, Eagle, and Owl. As soon as the race began, Fish left the starting line and flopped back into the creek. Squirrel climbed a tree and jumped from tree to tree trying to reach the finish line. Both Eagle and Owl cheated by flying through the air. Rabbit won the race. He was a star. He ran to the top of the hill and back as fast as he could go, and, oh, it felt good. Rabbit said to himself, "I can't believe it. At school, I get to do what I do best."

The instructor said, "Rabbit, you really have a talent for running. You've great muscles in your rear legs. With some training, you'll get more out of every hop."

Little Rabbit said, "I love school. I get to do what I like to do and learn to do it better."

The next class was swimming. Little Rabbit looked into the creek and said, "Wait, wait! Rabbits don't like to swim."

The instructor said, "Little Rabbit, you need a well-rounded education. You may not like swimming now, but five years from now you'll know it was a good thing for you."

Fish and Duck loved the swimming class, but Little Rabbit, Squirrel, Eagle, and Owl left the water.

For the tree-climbing class, a tree trunk was set at a 30-degree angle so all the animals had a chance to succeed. Little Rabbit tried so hard to climb the tree, but his legs hurt.

In jumping class, Little Rabbit and Squirrel got along just fine; in flying class, Little Rabbit and Squirrel had problems. So the teacher gave them a test and discovered they belonged in remedial flying. In remedial flying class, Little Rabbit and Squirrel practiced jumping off a cliff. The instructor told them, "If you just work hard enough, you'll succeed."

The next morning, school started with swimming class. The instructor said, "Today we jump into the water."

Little Rabbit and Squirrel complained, "Our parents said we don't need to swim. They didn't learn to swim. We don't like to get wet. I'd like to drop this course."

The instructor said, "You can't drop it. You must have a well rounded education. You have a choice: either you jump in or you flunk."

Little Owl quit school. His mother decided to do home schooling.

Little Rabbit and Squirrel jumped into the creek. Squirrel panicked! Squirrel went down once. Squirrel went down twice. Bubbles came up. The instructor saw Squirrel was drowning and pulled him out. The other animals had never seen anything quite as funny as wet Little Rabbit and wet Squirrel. Little Rabbit looked like a long eared wet rat without a tail. Squirrel looked like a wet rat with a long tail. Fish, Duck and Eagle chirped, jumped, and laughed at Rabbit and Squirrel. Rabbit was more humiliated than he had ever been in his life. He wanted desperately to get out of class that day. He was glad when school was out.

Little Rabbit thought that his parents would understand and help him. When he arrived home, he told his parents, "I don't like school. I just want to be free."

His parents told him, "Rabbits must get an education and a diploma it they are to get ahead. You've got to stay in school and get a diploma."

Little Rabbit said, "I don't want a diploma."

His parents answered, "You're going to stay in school and get a diploma whether you want one or not."

They argued, and finally his parents made Little Rabbit go to bed. In the morning, Little Rabbit headed off to school with a slow hop-hop-hop. Then he remembered what the counselor had said, "Any time a student has a problem, the counselor's door is always open, so come see me."

Little Rabbit arrived at school, he hopped up in the chair in the counselor's office and said, "I don't like school."

The counselor said, "Mmmm, tell me about it."

Little Rabbit told the counselor his problems with school.

The counselor replied, "Little Rabbit, I hear you. I hear you saying you don't like school because you don't like swimming, climbing trees, or flying. I think I've diagnosed that correctly. Little Rabbit, I tell you what we'll do. You're doing great in running and hopping. You don't need to work on your running. What you need to work on is swimming, climbing, and flying. I'll arrange it so you don't have to go to running or jumping class anymore. You'll have two periods of swimming, two periods of climbing, and tutoring after school on flying. I'll put Squirrel in remedial running, and he'll be with you in your swimming classes."

Little Rabbit had a frown on his face when he hopped out of the counselor's office. Little Rabbit looked up and saw the mother of a friend, Mrs. Wise Owl. Mrs. Wise Owl cocked her head and said, "Little Rabbit, life doesn't have to be that way. We could have schools and businesses where people are allowed to concentrate on what they do best."

Little Rabbit was inspired. He thought when he graduated, he would start a school where rabbits concentrated on running and hopping, squirrels would concentrate on climbing trees, fish would concentrate on swimming, and ducks would concentrate on swimming and flying.

MISER'S USELESS GOLD

Miser did not trust banks nor paper dollars the government printed. Every weekend, Miser was paid for his week's work. Miser immediately swapped his dollar bills for gold coins. Then Miser took his new gold coins and deposited them into an old cedar chest. Every weekend, Miser sat looking and gloating over his gold coin treasure.

Thief became aware that Miser bought gold coins every week and took them home. Thief spied on Miser. One weekend night, after Miser gloated over his treasurers, Thief saw Miser hide the cedar chest with his gold coin treasure.

The next weekend, Miser came home to add his weekly gold coins to his cedar chest treasure and gloat over it; Miser found nothing but an empty cedar chest. His gold coin treasure had disappeared. Miser called the police. Neighbors heard about Miser's tragedy. One neighbor visited Miser. Miser told his neighbor about his tragedy and described how he spent every weekend counting and examining his gold coin treasure.

The neighbor asked Miser, "Did you ever take any gold coin out and spend them?"

Miser answered, "Oh no. I guarded my gold coin treasure, so I could look at it every weekend."

The neighbor advised, "Continue to look at your cedar chest every weekend. It'll do you just as much good as the gold coin did before."

MOST IMPORTANT TEST

It was the week of final exams at the university. Test results determined if students failed, passed, or excelled. Test results determined if some students graduated, if others entered graduate school, or if some obtained their dream jobs.

The university intended that a certain chemistry course filter out students who didn't have the ability to attend med school, or vet school, or pharmacy school, or graduate studies in science. Some years, more than half the class failed.

The students saw the chemistry course as a potential dream crusher. A young lady dreamed of becoming a doctor. The final exam determined if she would be in med school next year, or if she would teach high school science. A young man dreamed of owning a veterinarian clinic. The final exam determined if he would be in vet school next year or, if he would ask his father to help him get a job at the local bank. Another student dreamed of graduating next week, and then working at a resort during the summer. The final exam determined if he graduated next week, or if he returned for summer school.

The chemistry professor held the final exam in his hands. Before distributing the exam, the professor told his students, "Today you are being tested for both chemistry and honesty. I hope you pass both tests. However, if you must fail one, fail chemistry. Many good people can't pass a chemistry test; however, no one who fails the honesty test is a good person."

NEW MD

A baby boy was born in the slums in a certain third world country. His mother was poor. The boy never knew his father. The future appeared bleak. The boy would probably become another criminal his slum was famous for producing. However, the boy studied hard, graduated from high school, university, and medical school. Then he married. She wasn't a beauty, but he loved her and she loved him.

The new couple moved to a small town, a long, long way from the city where he completed his medical studies. The town rejoiced to receive its first doctor. The young doctor opened his medical office. It was small and only had the bare necessities. But it was his office. One night a desperate man knocked on the door of the doctor's home. The man's wife was giving birth to a baby. The birth was complicated and the local mid-wife needed help.

The new MD threw tools into his medical bag and hurried after the father. It was the woman's first baby. It was the doctor's first delivery. The couple lived on the second floor above a bakery. The doctor ran up the stairs. The expectant father waited in the kitchen, smoking one cigarette after another.

The doctor opened his medical bag, grabbed one instrument, threw it away, gabbed another, threw it away. Medical instruments began to fly all over the room as he tried to remember the courses he had studied in the distant medical school. In desperation, he threw a tool that landed on the mothers head, fracturing her skull. The doctor realized the disaster, and he became more nervous. Finally he grabbed the baby by the head and pulled it out.

The desperate doctor took the baby to the father in the kitchen. The doctor didn't look where he was stepping and slipped on the uneven drop from the bedroom to the kitchen. He began to fall and dropped the baby. The father gave a desperate jump to catch the baby. The father caught the baby but couldn't stop before reaching the kitchen window. Father and baby plunged through the window.

The town rose up in anger. At home, the doctor's wife comforted her husband. The doctor and his wife left in the middle of the night to move to another town a long, long, long way away. Another office. Another town excited to have its first doctor. Another mother giving birth. Another nervous father knocking on the door in the middle of the night. The doctor ran to their home. The doctor returned home and his wife asked if things went better that time. The doctor replied, "Yep, this time I saved the father."

NIGHT WATCHMAN

I was traveling with my wife and Pastor Marcos, a Brazilian pastor friend, going from Brasilia to Rio de Janeiro. We were going to lead Bible Storytelling Training clinics, and I was towing a trailer full of books. The highway was full of potholes. I continued driving after sunset. In the darkness of night, I entered a pothole and ruined a tire. We had difficulty changing the tire in the darkness. Shortly afterwards we discovered a small hotel, very simple, yet clean. When I was registering, I told the clerk, "My car and trailer are full of books; do I need to remove them, or do you have a night watchman?"

The clerk answered: "We have a night watchman," and pointed toward a man sitting outside in a chair.

Early the following morning, I slipped out of bed, leaving my wife asleep in order to buy a new tire before breakfast. But the front door of the hotel was locked, and I could not find an exit. Finally, I found a young lady in the kitchen preparing breakfast. I asked her how to get out. She answered: "The night watchman has the only key, and he gets up at seven o'clock."

The man sitting outside the hotel had the title of night watchman. He earned the salary of a night watchman. He looked like a night watchman. But he did not fulfill his job of staying awake and watching the cars.

In John's gospel, chapter ten, Jesus speaks about the mercenary who looks like a shepherd, has the responsibility of taking care of the sheep, but who does not do the job if a wolf appears. He is not willing to risk his life to protect the sheep. Regretfully, there are men who have the title of pastor, receive the salary of a pastor, but when they are unobserved, do not fulfill the job of a pastor.

"NO" FROM LOVED ONES

Child: "Daddy, can I play ball in the street?"
Daddy: "No!"

Child: "Mama, can I play with matches?"
Mama: "No!"

Child: "Mama, look, there is a big rope in the yard. Look it's wiggling and moving. Can I play with the big rope?"
Mama: "No!"

Child: "Daddy, can I ride my bike to the river and go swimming?"
Daddy: "No!"

Child: "Daddy, that man on the street corner by the school gives children free candy, can I have some?"
Daddy: "No!"

Child: "Mother, I've made a new friend on the internet. He wants to meet me at the mall. Can I go to the mall by myself and meet him?"
Mother: "No!"

Child: "I don't want to do my homework. I want to watch TV!"
Mother: "No. No TV until your homework is done!"

Child: "Daddy, Let me use the computer to talk to my friends on MySpace. Don't make me do my homework."
Daddy: "No!"

Child: "Daddy, Let me play with your electric drill?"
Daddy: "No!"

Child: "Daddy, can I try a cigarette?"

Daddy: “No!”

Child: “Daddy, I don’t feel like making up my bed like mama said. I want to go out and play. Can you give me some money?”

Daddy: “No!”

Child: “Mama, I want a pair of tennis shoes just like Hannah Montana. They only cost $450.”

Mama: “No!”

Child: “Mama, can I put the tweezers into the wall socket?

Mama: “No!”

Child: “Daddy, let me get onto the bridge and throw rocks at the cars on the street below?”

Daddy: “No!”

Child: “Mama and Daddy. What can I do? You won’t let me do anything I wanna do. If you loved me, you’d let me do what I want to do.”

Daddy: “We love you. Because we love you, we won’t let you do many things that you want to do.”

OLD PREACHER'S STORY

An elderly preacher retired from pastoring a local church, but he did not retire from ministry. Every week he took his Bible to visit prisoners locked up in the county jail.

One week the elderly pastor visited the jail and introduced himself to new prisoners. A young prisoner told the elderly preacher, "Don't waste your time on me. There's no hope for me."

The preacher responded, "I'm not ready to give up on you. There's still hope for you."

The prisoner answered, "Preacher, leave me alone. I'm no good. Everybody I touched became damaged goods. I damaged everybody who ever cared about me. My mother is sick with worry. I abused my wife and daughter when I was drunk or on drugs. I turned my little brother into a drug dealer."

The preacher answered, "You've done serious harm. The wounds you inflicted on others may take a long time to heal. They'll leave permanent scars. But you can find a new path. Let me tell you a story."

The young prisoner cursed and shouted, "A story!" I'm desperate, and you wanna tell me a stupid story. I've no hope and you wanna tell me a story with a happy ending. I'm gonna spend the rest of my life behind bars. I need new facts, but I don't need fiction!"

The elderly preacher replied, "Do me a favor. Let this old preacher tell you a story."

The old preacher told his story: "Once upon a time several heroes of Heaven were together. Among those present were Noah, Abraham, Moses, David, Peter, the Samaritan woman who met Jesus at a well, Paul, and Dr. Luke. The window of Heaven was open. Heaven's heroes observed an old preacher entering a county jail. Someone in Heaven asked, "Why's that old preacher wasting his time with those wicked prisoners? There's no hope for any of them!"

Noah spoke up, "I can't say there is no hope for those prisoners. I'm not the man to judge those prisoners. I can't even defend myself. God saved me and my family through the flood. Then I got drunk and passed out naked in my tent. My youngest son told my two older sons about my condition. I was so angry with my youngest son that I put a curse on his son, my grandson. It's only by God's grace that I'm in heaven."

Abraham spoke up, "I can't say there is no hope for those prisoners. I'm not the man to judge those prisoners. I can't even defend myself. When there was a famine in Canaan, I didn't consult God, I took my wife and headed to Egypt. As we entered Egypt, I told my wife, 'Honey, you're a beautiful woman. They might kill me to get to you. Don't tell them you're my wife, tell them you're my sister.' I lied to save my life and I put my wife's honor at risk. It's only by God's grace that God made me a blessing to all nations."

Moses spoke up, "I can't say there is no hope for those prisoners. I'm not the man to judge those prisoners. I can't even defend myself. I was forty years old, and I saw an Egyptian man mistreating one of my Jewish relatives. I murdered that Egyptian in cold blood and hid his body in the sand. It's only by God's grace that God chose me to free the Jews from slavery in Egypt and lead them to the Promised Land."

King David spoke up, "I can't say there is no hope for those prisoners. I'm not the man to judge those prisoners. I can't even defend myself. One spring, I should have led my army into battle, but I stayed home in Jerusalem. One day after lunch, I took a nap. Then I walked up to the flat roof of my palace. From the vantage point of my roof, I saw a beautiful woman taking a bath. I knew that her husband was one of my mighty warriors, but I sent for her and went to bed with her. She became pregnant, and I ordered my commander-in-chief to send her husband to the front line of battle. I murdered her husband by my enemy's sword. My actions caused many people to lose any respect for God. It's only by God's grace that I'm forgiven and one of my descendants became the Messiah."

The Samaritan woman spoke up, "I can't say there is no hope for those prisoners. I'm not the woman to judge those prisoners. I can't even defend myself. My first husband didn't satisfy my desires, so I divorced him and married another. My second husband didn't satisfy me, and I swapped him. After five husbands, I was an outcast in my own village. I couldn't get another man to marry me, but I found a man to live with me. It's only by God's grace that Jesus offered me living water that satisfied a thirst that men couldn't satisfy."

Peter spoke up, "I can't say there is no hope for those prisoners. I'm not the man to judge those prisoners. I can't even defend myself. I walked with Jesus for three years and heard all the stories He told. Jesus invited me to pray with Him in the garden, but I went to sleep. When Jesus was on trial for His life, I was a coward and denied that I knew Him three different times. It's only by God's grace that Jesus restored me as a disciple and used me to cast the Gospel-net as a fisherman of people."

Paul spoke up, "I can't say there is no hope for those prisoners. I'm not the man to judge those prisoners. I can't even defend myself. I was a religious fanatic. I persecuted believers in Jesus and tried to destroy the church by having followers of Jesus arrested and put to death. It's only by God's grace that Jesus saved me and used me to preach about Jesus and plant churches in distant places."

Dr. Luke spoke up. "I didn't do any of the things you people confessed. People called me, "The Good Doctor." But I recorded stories Jesus told about the lost sheep that the Good Shepherd carried home and the younger prodigal brother who was welcomed home by his father. I also recorded true stories such as the following: Jesus forgave the prostitute who poured perfume over His feet; Jesus justified His eating with sinners and social outcasts by saying the healthy don't need a doctor, but the sick do; and Jesus said He came to seek and save sinners. I recorded many stories about God's grace toward sinners and social outcasts."

The old preacher concluded, "I wanna tell you stories, not as an exercise in fiction, but because I want you to take the stories I tell you and experience them as your story."

ONLY A MOTHER

This is a non-fiction crafted story. It's based on facts; however, I used my imagination to embellish the facts, reinvent situations, create dialogue, and fill in unavailable facts. Dr. Alexander Sapiro gave me permission to tell this story.

Alexander Sapiro was born in Romania in 1946. He was six years old, in 1952, when his parents immigrated to Brazil. His family was fleeing from both communism and the poverty of one of the poorest countries in Europe. After arriving in Brazil, little Alexander's parents lived in a colony with other immigrants from Romania. Everyone in the colony spoke their native language of Romanian. Romanian is derived from Latin and is in the same linguistic family as Portuguese; nevertheless, Alexander's parents had difficulty speaking and understanding Portuguese. Children from the colony went to Brazilian schools and were forced to learn Portuguese. Families in Alexander's colony were proud of their children who completed the Brazilian high school. Students who got into a university were considered heroes. The elders told the university student, "Education is power."

Alexander's father became a diabetic before there were instruments to monitor glucose levels in the blood. Those instruments became available in the 1970's. At that time, there were no "light" nor "diet" foods. Diabetes was treated with some oral medication, insulin, diet, and exercise. The basic treatment for Alexander's father consisted of two things: his mother did not use sugar when she cooked, and his father took insulin shots.

Determining the blood glucose or sugar content was done by putting a urine sample in a test tube with the proper amount of Benedict's Reagent's Chemical Powder. When heated, the chemical reaction caused the color to change from blue if glucose was presence. The color change indicated whether the sugar content was high, low, or normal. This was a complicated task. It was an impossible task for Alexander's parents who had difficulty understanding the doctor's instructions in Portuguese.

Alexander was in fourth grade in a Brazilian school. He understood the doctor's instructions better than his parents. It became Alexander's duty to test the sugar content of his father's urine on a daily basis. Alexander accompanied his father on visits to the doctor's office because his father couldn't understand the doctor. At home, the boy helped his father follow the doctor's instructions.

The frequent visits to the doctor with his father, and the responsibility of supervising his father's medical care inspired Alexander to become a doctor. He wanted to help others with diabetes, the same way the doctor was helping his father.

Dr. Alexander Sapiro finished medical school in 1970 and began his residence in pediatrics at a children's hospital called Hospital da Criança Santo Antônio in the city of Porto Alegro. Several times, Dr. Sapiro attended a small boy named Pedro in the emergency room. Pedro lived with his parents on a farm, a great distance away from the city. Pedro was diabetic. When Pedro's sugar count was out of control, his mother, Dona Maria, walked four miles from their small farm to the village. If Dona Maria's husband was using the donkey to haul farm produce, and if Pedro was too sick to walk, Dona Maria carried Pedro in her arms for four miles. Only a mother would carry a sick child for four miles. Other times, Dona Maria walked beside the donkey, supporting Pedro who sat on the donkey. In the village, they would catch a bus that took three hours to reach the city of Porto Alegro. From the bus station, they took another city bus to the hospital. Only a mother would have gone to so much trouble for a sick little boy.

Dona Maria was illiterate. Dr. Sapiro felt sure she did not understand his complicated instructions, "First thing every morning, collect one-half ounce of Pedro's urine in this test tube, pour in ½ teaspoon of this Benedict's Reagent's Chemical Powder, and heat the tube until all the liquid inside has the same color. If the color changes from blue, consult this color chart to determine the level of sugar." Remarkably, Dona Maria did a good job of controlling the situation. She only brought Pedro to the hospital when his sugar count was out of control. Dr. Sapiro thought, "Maybe there's an old wives' method of determining when sugar count is out of control. Dona Maria could teach me a method that I could use to instruct the unschooled, who can't follow my instructions on using chemicals, test tubes, and color charts to monitor glucose levels."

Dr. Sapiro asked Dona Maria how she determined when Pedro's sugar count was out of control. Dr. Sapiro discovered that Dona Maria did not use the test tube. First thing each morning Dona Maria took a sip of her son's urine. She knew how sweet it should taste. When it tasted too sweet, Dona Maria rushed to take Pedro to the hospital.

Only a mother would go to so much trouble for a sick little child. Only a mother.

PANCAKE DISASTER

Six-year-old, Douglas, and his five-year-old sister, Carol, always got up early on Saturdays while their parents slept late.

One Saturday the children decided to surprise their parents and fix them pancakes. Carol found a big bowl and a spoon. Douglas pulled a chair to the counter, opened the cupboard and pulled out the flour canister, spilling it on the floor. The counter was too high for them, so they put their work on the floor. Douglas and Carol got on their knees and used their hands to scoop up half of the flour into the bowl. The rest was left on the floor. Carol got milk from the refrigerator while Douglas returned to the cupboard for a canister of sugar. They poured in milk and sugar, without measuring. Some of each was spilled on the floor. They left a floury trail on the floor to the refrigerator and the cupboard.

The dog came to investigate the noise and stayed to help, and he added to the floury tracks. Carol remembered that Mama always put eggs into the pancakes. She got eggs out of the refrigerator, but tripped over the dog, dropping the egg carton on the floor. Carol and Douglas scooped up some of the eggs and put them into the bowl.

Carol said they needed to clean up before cooking the pancakes. She got on her knees to clean up the mess, getting sticky eggs and flour all over her pajamas. Douglas went to figure out how the stove worked. Then the children noticed the dog was eating from the bowl. They scolded the dog, and he ran through the house, tracking the mess into other rooms. Carol said the pancakes went into the oven, Douglas thought they were cooked on top of the stove. Douglas couldn't figure out how to work the stove and decided to help his sister clean up. They both got sticky eggs and flour all over their pajamas.

The brother and sister wanted to do something special for Mama and Daddy, but things were getting very bad. Crocodile tears welled up in Carol and Douglas' eyes. They had wanted to do something good but had made a terrible mess. They were afraid what would happen when Mama and Daddy got up. They feared Mama and Daddy getting mad, and they might get a spanking. Then they saw Daddy standing at the door. The brother and sister began to sob. The father stood watching for over a minute while the children's sobs grew louder. Then their daddy walked through the mess with bare feet, sat down in the middle of the sticky mess and put his arms around his two sobbing children to hug, comfort and love them.

TOXIC PARENTS ANGRY AT DAUGHTER

Our family lived in Brasilia, the capital city of Brazil. A young newly married couple started attending a weekly Bible study my wife and I were leading in an apartment. Someone in the group mentioned to me that the young lady's father was a famous senator with ambitions to enter the next presidential race. However, the young lady never mentioned her family. Then one week she did.

One week, the young lady was visibly upset and shared with the group that her parents had strongly criticized her for bringing shame on the family by wearing a two-piece swimsuit at a pool party.

We heard her story and first thought that the young lady's parents didn't approve of women wearing two-piece swimsuits.

The young lady corrected us and said, "No! No–no. When I was fifteen years old, I slipped out of the house and went to a party without telling my parents. My daddy found out I went to the party and he tied my arms around a tree and beat me with a belt. I refused to promise Daddy I'd never slip out of the house again. Daddy went to the barn and returned with a horse whip. My parents accused me of bringing shame on my family by wearing a two piece swimsuit that allowed people to see scars on my back from the multiple whippings Daddy gave me. They said I'm a disgrace to the family, and my shameful actions help his enemies, and it'll be my fault if he doesn't advance in his political career."

PASTOR SEARCH COMMITTEE'S REPORT

The church's long time Senior Pastor retired. The church elected a Pastor Search Committee to filter through recommendations for a new pastor and to recommend a candidate to become the new Senior Pastor for the church.

The Pastor Search Committee took six months before making its report to the church. This is their report:

The Pastor Search Committee received many recommendations of candidates to be considered for the position of Senior Pastor of our church. We investigated the following candidates that different church members recommended. The following are candidates we seriously considered and our observations on each one.

Noah:

- Has 120 years of preaching experiences, without a single convert
- Background check reveals he was investigated for drunkenness, indecent exposure, and cursing at his home

Abraham:

- Too old for the job. He was seventy-five-years old when he responded to God's call
- During a time of drought, he went to Egypt and was expelled from the country because he lied to government officials
- Has a child with his wife's maid

Moses:

- Not an eloquent speaker – stammers
- His last congregation accused him of losing his patience and getting angry over little things

David:

- Had an affair; he has an unacceptable moral character
- If he hadn't had his moral failure, we'd recommend him for the position of Minister of Music

Solomon:

- Has a reputation for being a wise man; however, he also has a reputation for not practicing what he preaches

Elijah:

- Constantly had conflict with government authorities
- Intolerantly cruel to leaders of different religious persuasions
- Periodically suffers depression

Amos:

- A country-hick, hillbilly with little education
- Wants to preach in the city, but in our opinion he should return to the hill country

Hosea:

- Married a prostitute and has a dysfunctional family
- Divorced

Jeremiah:

- Very emotional
- Constantly warns of pending disaster
- Accused of being a traitor to our nation

John the Baptist:

- His sermons condemn everyone
- Shows no respect to religious leaders
- Dresses like a hippie and gives no attention to proper etiquette

John the Apostle:

- Because of his violent temper, nicked-named, "Son of Thunder"

- On more than one occasion, showed intolerance toward people of other races
- Claims to have a special relationship with Jesus

Peter:
- Speaks before thinking
- His desire to please people has resulted in inconsistency
- He keeps repeating the same mistakes
- Once publicly denied knowing Jesus

Paul:
- Hard-headed. Critical of church leaders who disagree with him
- Had several conflict situations that resulted in his being run out of town
- Been in jail three or four times; however, he claims he is innocent of any crime
- Never stays at a place longer than three years
- Preaches very, very long sermons
- Not good at record keeping, doesn't remember some people he baptized
- Health problems

Timothy:
- A young man with potential, but he's too young for our church
- Very timid and lacks courage
- Lacks creativity, constantly repeats sermons and writings of Paul

Judas:
- Good with finances
- Team player
- Recognized as a leader by co-workers. Judas criticized Mary for wasting money when she poured expensive perfume on Jesus; his co-workers followed his leadership
- Expresses concern for the poor
- Sharp dresser

Your Pastor Search Committee has reached an unanimous decision to recommend Judas as the best man to become Senior Pastor of our church.

PASTOR'S CONFESSION

Pastor Billy Bob Backer was the beloved pastor of Red Rock Baptist Church located on County Road 24. It was the custom in Billy Bob's county for pastors to gather on Monday mornings to fellowship and to pray together.

One Monday morning, Billy Bob went to the pastors meeting. Several pastors shared experiences from their church on Sunday. One pastor asked Billy Bob, "How were things at your church yesterday? Anything exciting happen?"

Billy Bob answered, "Didn't go to church yesterday."

The pastors showed concern and asked Billy Bob if he had been sick.

Pastor Billy Bob answered, "I was sick at heart. When I was a child, a Bulldog bit me, and I'm terrified of big dogs. But I have a neighbor with two Pit Bull dogs. He lets his dogs run free. I've asked him several times to keep his dogs off my property, but he claims they are tame and no danger. Saturday, both of his dogs came into my yard and my son ran to play with them. It terrified me; I had a panic attack. I screamed and threw rocks at the dogs to run them off my property. My neighbor saw me throwing rocks at his dogs and started arguing with me. I got so mad at him that I used curse words that I used before I became a Christian. I cursed him out. I told him that if his dogs came into my yard again I'd use my gun next time. I was ready to fight him when my wife grabbed my arm and pulled me into the house.

"I realized I was in no condition to preach yesterday. I called a deacon to take care of the worship service. Yesterday morning, I got up before sunrise and took off in my car. I drove and drove and drove. I didn't go to church. I got home after dark and apologized to my wife for my behavior and for embarrassing her. I apologized to my son for losing my temper and using curse words and I apologize to you, my fellow preachers, for my behavior. I gave my neighbor, and everyone he talks to, cause to use the argument, 'If the preacher lives a lie, how can we believe he preaches the truth.' Pray for me because tonight I'm going to my neighbor and apologize for my actions and words. And next Sunday, I'll apologize to the church for not practicing what I preach."

The preachers ended the meeting by placing Pastor Billy Bob Backer in a chair and all the pastors gathered around him in a circle to pray for him.

Each preacher left the meeting aware that an angry reaction to someone's words or actions could damage his potential for serving Christ.

TAKING PAVEMENT TO HEAVEN

A baby boy was born to Mr. and Mrs. Penton. His parents called him Robert Andrew Penton. However, everyone called him Bobby. His parents started taking Bobby to church when he was a baby in their arms. When Bobby became a young boy, sometimes his parents would stay home on Sundays, but even then they would drive Bobby to church and pick him up afterwards.

Bobby was sixteen years old when his parents gave him a second-hand car, the car that his mother had been driving. His parents told Bobby, "We've always insisted you go to church, but now we are going to leave the choice to you. You can continue if you wish, or you can stop going."

Bobby answered, "I believe in God, I believe the Bible to be the Word of God, I believe God answers prayers, and I enjoy going to church. I'll continue going to church."

Bobby prayed that God would help him make good grades in high school, and he made the honor roll. Then Bobby prayed that God would help him obtain a scholarship to a prestigious university; an elite university offered Bobby an academic scholarship.

Bobby went to the university and introduced himself as Robert. Robert prayed that he would make good grades. He made the Dean's List. Robert was in his sophomore year, and he prayed that he would find a girlfriend who would make him a good wife. Robert fell in love with Laura, a beautiful, talented, young lady who also loved God and loved the church. During his senior year, Robert prayed that he would find a job where he could afford to get married. He sent out resumes and went to job fairs. Robert was offered a good paying job for someone just out of college. He would start to work a month after graduation. Robert prayed that Laura would be willing to be his fiancee. Laura said, "Yes!" Robert and Laura became engaged.

The week after graduating from the university, Robert and Laura were married. Robert maxed out his credit cards paying for their honeymoon, first month's rent in a furnished apartment, and food until his first paycheck. Robert prayed that he would be able to pay off his credit card debts within a year; he payed them off in eleven months. Robert was still driving the car his parents gave him for his sixteenth birthday, and he prayed to be able to buy their first new car. He was able to buy and make payments on a new SUV. Then Robert prayed that he would get a job promotion so they could afford to buy a house. The promotion came, and they bought their own home.

Then Robert prayed that God would give Laura and him children. First came a baby boy; two years later a baby girl was born.

Then Robert prayed for another promotion so they could afford a larger home with yard space where the children could play, and in a community with excellent schools. With the promotion, people at work started calling him "Mr. Robert Penton." Mr. and Mrs. Robert Penton were able to buy a larger home in a more expensive neighborhood that had an outstanding school system. Each time Mr. Robert Penton prayed for a promotion, he was promoted. When the president of the company retired, Mr. Penton prayed that the job would be his; Mr. Robert Penton became the company's president.

Mr. Robert Penton kept praying for his children: that they would be healthy, that they would do well in school, that they would get into elite universities, that they would make good choices when they married, and that his children would make he and Laura grandparents. Each of the things Robert prayed for happened.

Mr. Penton was fifty-nine years old when he was diagnosed with terminal lung cancer. The doctor said he probably had four months to live, six months at the most. Mr. Penton prayed, "God, I know they say you can't take it with you, but you've answered all my prayers. I want to be able to take my wealth with me. Now Lord, you know I got to be president of the company by working hard, being honest, and putting in long hours. I didn't step on people's backs to climb the ladder of success. I did my best for the company and I prayed for you to open the doors of opportunity. So, let me take my wealth with me."

Mr. Robert Penton felt sure that God gave him an affirmative answer. Mr Penton searched his Bible and he could not find any mention of stocks and bonds, nor dollars in Heaven. But he found several mentions of gold in Heaven. So Mr. Penton ordered his broker to convert his stocks and bonds into gold and send it to his home. A full container of gold was shipped to Mr. Penton's home.

Mr. Penton reached the pearly gates of heaven and he met Saint Peter. Mr. Penton was so excited when he looked beyond the pearly gates and saw the container with his gold. Simon Peter's brother, Andrew, was watching when Robert Penton excitedly opened his container of gold.

Later Andrew asked Peter, "Was Robert Penton able to bring his wealth to Heaven in that container?"

Peter answered, "Yes, that container contains all his wealth."

Andrew asked, "What was in it? Does it contain records of sick people he visited?"

Peter answered, "No."

Andrew asked, "Does it contain records of the hungry people he fed, the poor he helped, the needy he helped get jobs, the under-privileged children he tutored, the mistreated for whom he obtained justice?"

Peter answered, "No, no, no, no, no."

Andrew asked, “Does it contain the names of people who are coming here because he showed them the way?”

Peter answered, “No.”

Andrew asked, “Well, what is in the container?”

Peter answered, “Pavement, nothing but pavement!”

Andrew said, “I thought Robert Penton was a man who knew how to pray.”

Peter answered, “Oh yes, Robert Penton knew how to pray with faith, and God answered his prayers. However, his prayers were always about himself, his wife, his two children, those four and no more. His prayers of faith were sweet perfume reaching up to God. But God always waited for more from Robert’s prayers. He wanted to see Robert Penton use his prayers to bring blessings to others.”

Andrew asked, “Well, what are we going to do with all that gold? The main streets of heaven are already paved. The streets that pass in front of the mansions are paved, and so are the streets that pass in front of the cottages.”

Peter answered, “I’ve already talked to the Lord about it. The Lord said we can pave the path that goes up to the travel trailer that will be Robert Penton’s home in glory.”

PENCIL COMPARED TO A PERSON

The grandparents were visiting. Little Johnny wanted to listen to his grandfather's stories; however, Little Johnny's mother said he had to do his homework first.

Little Johnny sat chewing on his pencil. His granddaddy sat in a chair, reading a book, waiting for Little Johnny to finish his homework. Johnny spoke, "I can't do it. This is too hard."

Granddaddy asked, "What's the trouble son. Maybe I can help."

Little Johnny said, "This is too hard. It's ridiculous. The teacher said for us write a paper making a comparison between a person and some object."

Granddaddy asked, "Have you come up with an object to compare to people?"

Little Johnny answered, "No, I can't think of anything!" Then he threw his pencil down on the floor.

Granddaddy said, "Don't be angry son. You'll never get your homework done. Why don't you compare a person to a pencil?" Granddaddy stooped over, picked up the pencil and gave it to Little Johnny.

Little Johnny asked, "How could I compare a pencil to people?"

Granddaddy answered, "We are like the pencil son. And God should be the hand that holds us and writes with us. When God gets angry, you wouldn't want him to throw you down the way you threw down the pencil, would you?"

Little Johnny felt embarrassed.

Granddaddy continued, "For a pencil to write, it is necessary to keep sharpening it, right?"

Little Johnny answered, "Sure, you gotta sharpen it for it to write."

Granddaddy continued, "For the pencil to stay sharp, you gotta use the pencil sharpener that cuts it."

Johnny answered, "Yea, that's right."

Granddaddy said, "For people to improve, its necessary to sharpen them. That is what parents and teachers do when they call attention to improper behavior. It's what they do when they punish a child for doing wrong. Most adults don't punish children because they are mean, they do it to help children become good adults."

Little Johnny said, "Well, yea, but what you gonna say about the color of the pencil?"

Granddaddy answered, "Color doesn't matter. The least important thing about a pencil is the way it looks. If the outside of a pencil is red, yellow, blue, or green, it continues to write because its lead is black."

Little Johnny responded, "So what is important is what is inside of each person. The lead is kind of like the heart. If the pencil is pretty on the outside, but the lead is weak, it's not much good for writing."

Granddaddy said, "That's right Johnny. There are also a lots of things you can do with a pencil. You can sketch a picture, doodle, write love letters, write dirty jokes, tell lies about people, and write profound truths."

Johnny said, "Just like we can do a lot of things with our lives. There are kids in my class who only use their pencils to write cruel notes to others, or they write trash on the walls. They make the teacher mad."

Granddaddy said, "Yes Johnny, we need to be careful what we do with our pencil."

Little Johnny said, "And Granddaddy, when we write with a pencil and make a mistake, we can use the rubber to erase it."

Granddaddy said, "Yes Johnny, most of the time, when we make a mistake in life, we can correct it and began again. But when we try to erase a mistake, it does leave smudge marks."

Little Johnny realized that he already had a lot to write about how a person can be compared to a pencil. He also thought about how his granddaddy was a worn out pencil who could still write beautiful words.

Little Johnny had a smile on his face when he took up his pencil and began to write about how a person can be compared to pencil.

POLICE – FEAR AND PREJUDICE

Eric Garner died in July 2014, when New York police officers held him in a choke hold and wrestled him to the ground. Eric's dying words, "I can't breathe," became a rallying cry against police brutality. In August 2014, Michael Brown, an unarmed teen, was shot to death in Ferguson, Missouri, during a confrontation with a police officer.

Protests erupted in many cities in the wake of decisions by grand juries not to indict those police officers in the deaths of two unarmed black men. Protesters crammed the streets and carried signs with the messages: "Black lives matter," "Hold cops accountable," and "I can't breathe."

May 25, 2020, a white police officer from Minneapolis crushed with his knee the neck of George Floyd, a black man, for 8 minutes and 46 seconds. George Floyd's dying words echoed Eric Garner's words in 2014, "I can't breathe."

Protest again erupted against brutal police actions against blacks. Rioters hijacked peaceful protests of George Floyd's death and turned them into riots – clashing with police, vandalizing stores, indulging in theft and arson, and spray-painting anti-police slogans on buildings.

Black Americans make up less than 13% of the United States population. However, black people are three times more likely to be killed by police than white people.

These events and facts got me thinking about my experiences with police officers. When I was a teenager in Enterprise, Alabama, some of my friends and I would stop by the police station to listen to some of the officers' stories. When I was in college, I went to a small church where a police officer's family often invited me and other students to their home for Sunday lunch. From that police officer, I picked up many of my ideas on how a man should treat his wife. Throughout the years I've had close friends who were police officers.

I've also had a few unpleasant encounters with the police. In 1963, I was a senior at a university in Birmingham, Alabama. One Sunday night, I was returning from my mother's home in Enterprise to Birmingham. I traveled through New Brockton and I ran a yellow signal light. A drunk policeman, who only used the bottom button on his shirt, stopped me and accused me of reckless driving. The drunk policeman kept my driver's license until I drove back home to Enterprise and returned with $40 in cash. That was a lot of money; my new 1962 Falcon cost $2047. Barber shops only charged $1.50 for a haircut. Family members later told me the cop had been fired from the Enterprise police department for drinking on the job. That cop was a bully with a badge.

For a few years, I lived in Fort Worth, Texas. One night, I was driving in Fort Worth and ran out of gas. This was years before cell phones. I was a jogger and ran a mile to a strip mall to use the pay phone booth to call friends for help. Two police cars raced up and four policemen exited their cars with hands on their guns. They shouted for me to raise my hands. They wanted to know why I was running through the strip mall after all the stores were closed. They didn't believe me when I told them my car ran out of gas and I ran to the strip mall to use a pay phone. The officers put me in the back seat of a police car and took me back to my car to verify my story. They justified their actions by saying I looked suspicious running through a strip mall after hours. They saw my car by the side of the road and left me by my car. I had to walk back a mile in the dark to the phone booth at the strip mall. I felt degraded and wronged. Those officers overreacted, and they were inconsiderate. They should have at least dropped me off by the phone booth where they first picked me up.

I, a white man, suffered from a bully with a badge and from inconsiderate cops who overreacted. I've heard black men describe similar experiences and claim that they experienced racially charged incidents with cops that point to a systemic racial problem with justice in America.

My son John has been vocally combative since childhood. When John was in elementary school, he researched books to prove his teachers wrong. When John was in the university, he punched a hole in his driver's license and put it on his key chain so he wouldn't need to carry a bill fold. A highway patrolman checked John's drivers license and accused John of destroying state property. John argued that there was no writing where he punched the hole. The patrolman threatened to arrest John for intentionally destroying state property. John laughed and said the policeman would look stupid before a judge. When John told me about the experience, I warned him, "Don't argue with police officers; they are powerful people. Police have the power to take someone's liberty away and put them in jail, solely at their discretion."

What we parents tell our children illustrates one of the defining differences between white and black America today. White parents warn our white sons to always cooperate with police officers because an officer could arrest them and put them in jail. Then they would be embarrassed and have a blemish on their record that could limit their opportunities for the future. Black parents warn their black sons to always show respect to police officers because even when they cooperate, an officer could kill them. What we parents tell our children illustrates one of the defining differences between white and black America today.

PRACTICE WHAT YOU PREACH

A certain preacher constantly preached powerful sermons, inspiring listeners to change their actions and grow in their relationship with God.

For many years the preacher observed an elderly gentleman who always sat on the second pew of the middle aisle of the church. The elderly gentleman soaked up every word the preacher said. He constantly took notes and commented to the preacher about his sermons. But one day, the elderly gentleman did not appear in church, and his seat forevermore remained vacant.

Years passed, and the pastor was coming to the end of his life. The pastor had a hard time letting go of this world and moving toward heaven. The pastor didn't want to leave this world. He suffered greatly in his efforts to hold onto his life, and he resisted death. The pastor couldn't discover the light to guide him during the passage from life on earth to life in heaven.

After days of struggle the pastor saw a person approaching him with a great light, and the person offered to help the pastor transition from earth to heaven. The pastor asked the person, "Who are you?"

The person answered, "Don't you remember me? I used to listen to your sermons every week." Then the pastor recognized the elderly gentleman who used to listen to him each week.

The pastor asked, "How did you get such a great light to guide you on the way?"

The man answered, "I believed the truths you preached and followed the advice you gave in your sermons."

The pastor realized that while he believed the truth, he hadn't always practiced the truth. He had preached the truth, but he hadn't always followed the counsel he preached. He had advised his listeners to lay up treasures in heaven while he was laying up treasures on earth.

REJECTED PRESENT

Old Man Duncan owned the hardware store in a small Southern town. Customers would enter his hardware store and tell Mr. Duncan what they needed, and he would fetch the supplies for them. Or a customer would tell Mr. Duncan the project he was working on, and Mr. Duncan would tell him the materials and tools needed and get them for him. If something broke, Mr. Duncan would explain how to fix it. If Old Man Duncan didn't have material, he'd order it and have it within three days. He'd explain to his customers how to do a job, or how to use the tools they were buying. He always remained calm and never lost his temper.

One morning, a half-back city slicker who had recently moved to the small town entered Duncan's hardware store. The locals called him a half-back because he had fled a northern city to get out of the harsh winters and had moved to Palm Beach, Florida. But he didn't like Florida's hurricanes, so he moved half-way back home and bought a house in the small Southern town. The half-back gave Old Man Duncan a list of materials he needed.

Old Man Duncan gathered the materials he had in stock, but there were a couple of items not in stock. Old Man Duncan explained, "I only sell some of these items about every six months. Don't keep them in stock. I'll order them; you can pick them up in three days."

The half-back ranted at the hardware store owner, "I don't want them in three days, I want them today. In the city, I can go to Lowes or Home Depot and get what I want when I want them."

The half-back raved and ranted. He cursed at Old Man Duncan for being inadequately stocked. He cursed at the small redneck town for the things it didn't have. Old Man Duncan calmly listened, remaining silent. Other customers waited for Mr. Duncan to loose his cool and tell the half-back where to go.

The half-back finally stormed out of the store. Another customer asked, "Why didn't you tell that arrogant half-back city slicker off? How did you keep silent? How could you not answer his unjust accusations against you?"

Old Man Duncan answered with a question, "If you offer me a present and I refuse it, who keeps the present?"

The customer answered, "Why, I keep the present. But what has this to do with those insults?"

Old Man Duncan replied, "That half-back offered me a present of various insults and curses that I refused to accept. Since I refused to accept them, he gets to keep them. When someone offers me a present of anger, insult, jealousy, greed – things that take away my peace of mind – I refuse it and let them keep it."

ROBBER DECEIVED

Raimundo was an undocumented immigrant. He lived and worked below the radar. He had no green card, no driver's license, no social security number, no health insurance, and no bank account. Raimundo had a university degree from his home country. But jobs were scarce and pay was little. Raimundo and his brother came to the USA to work for three years. They planned to make enough money in three years to buy and equip a computer store back in their home country. Ten people from their home country shared a two-bedroom-apartment. Raimundo and his brother shared the same bed. His brother worked days and slept nights. Raimundo worked nights and slept days.

Raimundo worked for a man who was contracted to clean a large office building at night. Every night, Raimundo did all the work cleaning the building. Every Saturday night, his boss showed up and paid Raimundo in cash, leaving no paper trail connecting Raimundo to his boss. Every Monday morning, Raimundo went to the bank and wired money home to his parents, who would then make a payment on the store Raimundo and his brother were buying.

One Sunday morning at 3 a.m., Raimundo finished cleaning the office building. He had cash from his week's wages in his side pocket. He locked the door to the office building and started walking through dimly lit streets to his apartment building. An armed robber stepped out of an alley between two abandoned buildings. He pointed his gun toward Raimundo and said, "Give me everything you got."

Raimundo slowly removed all his money from his pocket and gave it to the robber. The robber took the money and stuffed it into his torn Bermuda shorts. Then the robber said, "I want your rags too. Take them off."

Raimundo answered, "You want me to take off my clothes?"

The robber said, “Take them off!”

Raimundo removed his pants and shirt, and gave them to the robber. The robber removed his torn Bermuda shorts, discarded them onto the sidewalk, put on Raimundo’s pants and shirt, and fled.

Raimundo didn’t want to walk home in his underwear, so he put on the robbers discarded torn Bermuda shorts. Raimundo was an undocumented immigrant, so he was afraid to go to the police and report the robbery. Raimundo sauntered home to his apartment, woke his brother, and described his terrifying experience. He removed the robber’s torn Bermuda shorts to take a bath. He saw a bulge in the pockets of the Bermuda shorts. He checked to see what it was, and found his own money. When the robber removed his torn Bermuda shorts to put on Raimundo’s pants, he forgot to remove the stolen money from his torn Bermuda shorts.

ROOSTER AND THE DIAMOND

Proud Rooster was strutting in the backyard of the farmhouse watching over his hens. Rooster didn't understand people. Rooster asked himself, "Why do people bury seeds under the ground when seeds scattered above the grown would feed the chickens?"

Rooster observed the Farmer's wife planting a flower garden. Rooster asked himself, "Why do people plant flower seeds that grow plants that can't be eaten, when if they planted grain seeds, the seeds would produce grain the chickens could eat?"

Rooster observed everybody in Farmer's family on their knees by the flower garden, passing their hands over the ground, looking under leaves and sticks. But the people didn't pick up anything to put in their mouths to eat. Rooster heard people talking, "The diamond is so small....That diamond could be anywhere....Careful, don't step anywhere you haven't looked, or you'll bury the diamond under the ground."

Rooster didn't know that Farmer's daughter recently became engaged. The excited bride-to-be vowed never to remove her engagement ring from her finger. One Spring day, she helped her mother plant flowers in the flower garden, and the diamond from her engagement ring slipped out of its setting. All family members desperately searched around the flower garden for the diamond.

After the people left,. Rooster strutted over to the flower garden. Suddenly, Rooster spied something shining in the grass by the flower garden. The rooster checked it out to see if it was edible. It turned out to be the diamond that had slipped from its setting in the engagement ring.

Rooster had observed everybody in the family searching for the diamond. Rooster realized; he had found the diamond people were looking for. Rooster crowed, "You may be a treasure to people, but I'd rather have one grain of edible seed than a bucket full of diamonds."

SCISSORS AND NEEDLES

Mary Lou was a little girl when she learned to sew clothes, make quilts, and do needlework. Mary Lou's father and mother married shortly before he shipped off to war as a soldier. He never returned. Mary Lou's mother became a seamstress and supported herself by making clothes and doing needlework from a sewing room she had made out of the garage.

Mary Lou married George, a man who dedicated himself to advancing his business career. Home and family were the most important things to Mary Lou; however, advancing his career was the most important thing to George.

George didn't understand why Mary Lou made the children's clothes, or why she would mend torn clothes. George cut her down, "What are your scissors, needles, and cloth doing on the dining room table?"

Mary Lou asked George to spend more time with the children; George cut Mary Lou down, "Don't you know that I must make a living for all of you? I can't get ahead in business spending time at home."

George cut Mary Lou down for making the children's clothes and mending torn shirts and pants, "I make enough money; you don't need to waste your time sewing." Then an hour latter, George cut down Mary Lou again, "You waste too much money; cut back on expenses."

George cut down Mary Lou for nagging him to go see little Billy's little league baseball games. Finally George went to see a game. Little Billy went to bat three times. Little Billy got two hits; however, in the last inning, Little Billy struck out. Little Billy caught a fly ball that kept the other team from making a home run. The family got home and George made no comment about the two hits Billy made, nor the fly ball Billy caught.

George cut Billy down because he struck out the last time he was at bat.

Mary Lou wanted to talk to George about the children and a problem at school; George cut her off, “I’m too tired. I work all day. I face problems at work all day, can’t I at least get some peace and rest in my own home?” Then George would cut the children down because they had the TV on too loud, or they were making too much noise playing.

One rare night, George was at home before dinner; the children were playing, making lots of noise. George shouted at Mary Lou, “The one night I’m home you let the children run wild. I get no peace in my own home. Tell them to shut up. Get them out of the den and keep them out. Send them to their room, and don’t let them talk back to you!”

Mary Lou took the children to the kitchen, gave each a sandwich, then she took them to their bedroom, told them to play, and she closed the door.

Mary Lou went to the den with a pair of scissors and a needle in her hand. She told George, “We need to talk.”

George cut her off, “Not now. What I need is peace and quite in my own home!”

Mary Lou replied, “Yes, now.” She stood in front of George pointing her scissors and needle at him. Then she asked, “What can you do with scissors?”

George said, “With scissors? Why, you cut.”

Mary Lou asked, “And with a needle, what do you do?”

George replied, “Why, you sew.”

Mary Lou asked, “Could you make a shirt with just a pair of scissors? Can you mend a torn shirt with just a pair of scissors”

George cut her off, “How should I know? You know I don’t sew.”

Mary Lou responded, “I’m not playing, don’t you cut me off now! Can you make a shirt if you only use a pair of scissors?”

George responded, "Of course not."

Mary Lou continued, "To sew something, you must use both the scissors and the needle. When I'm sewing and little Sue wants to help me, I let her have a pair of children's scissors; she is satisfied to cut and cut and cut, until she cuts the cloth in such little pieces that they can't be used to make even doll clothes. Then I throw away what she cut as scraps.

"You know how to cut us down. You cut me for making clothes instead of buying them; you cut me for spending too much money; you cut me off when I want to talk to you; you cut the children for making too much noise; you cut the children off when they want to play with you; you cut Billy for striking out in baseball. If you keep cutting, you may find that you've cut us out of your life, and it'll be too late to sew the family back together. You need to learn when to cut and when to sew."

Then Mary Lou said, "I'm not going to say any more about it. I'm going to the children's room to give them some attention. I'll work on mending them where you cut them. Our family is too important for me to see it cut up and thrown away as scraps."

George didn't say anything when Mary Lou left the room. He sat still, thinking. About forty-five minutes later, George entered the children's bedroom. The children were playing, and Mary Lou was sitting on the floor with them. She had a needle and thread in her hands, mending a torn shirt as she watched them play. George realized he needed to work on mending his family. He asked Mary Lou and the children, "Would you like to go to McDonald's to get something to eat?"

SECOND TIME IN CHURCH

I saw Harvey in our church building for the first time on Wednesday evening. It was the first time he had ever been in church with his wife, children, grandchildren, and friends. Harvey was in his mid-seventies; his thinning gray hair was freshly cut, his mustache was trimmed, and he was wearing his best navy blue suit.

Harvey's wife, son, daughter-in-law, and grandchildren attended our church every Sunday and every Wednesday night, but I had never seen Harvey there. I knew that years ago, conflict had surrounded the wedding of Harvey's son and daughter-in-law. The mother of the bride wanted a big church wedding. Harvey, the father of the groom, said that if the wedding were held at church, he wouldn't attend. Harvey refused to give in to the pleading of his wife, his son, his son's fiancé, and his son's future in-laws. There was no compromise for Harvey, and the wedding was held in a rented reception hall.

Harvey loved his grandchildren. He took them fishing, and he went to every one of his grandson's ball games. However, he never came to church when his grandchildren sang in the children's program. He didn't come to church to see his grandchildren in the Christmas play. Harvey's granddaughter became a cheerleader for the high school basketball team, and Harvey went to every basketball game to watch her perform as a cheerleader. His granddaughter took voice lessons in high school and Harvey went to all the high school choir performances to listen to his granddaughter sing. However, when she sang solos at church, Harvey never came to hear her.

When his granddaughter became engaged, Harvey told her that if the wedding were at church, he would not go. Harvey's daughter-in-law did not give in to Harvey this time.

Harvey's daughter-in-law, and his granddaughter, the bride-to-be, wanted a big church wedding. Harvey's granddaughter's tears, his son's pleading, and his wife's arguments could not persuade Harvey to go to the wedding. In fact, the week before the wedding, Harvey went on a two-week fishing trip to get away from his nagging wife, who was constantly pleading with him to change his mind and go to their granddaughter's wedding.

Harvey also did not come to church for the funeral of his closest friend and neighbor.

Many times for breakfast or lunch, I sat at the big round table at the local café where local men often gather to eat and fellowship. Harvey was often at the table. Several times I invited him to visit our church. I knew that several of his Christian neighbors had talked to him about the Lord and had invited him to visit our church.

Harvey was respected. He was a faithful husband, a good father, a loving grandfather, an honest business man, and a neighbor who helped those in need. He had so many characteristics a Christian should have; however, he had never become a believer in Jesus, nor would he enter the doors of the church.

On one occasion, Harvey's son and daughter-in-law invited their friends and family to a barbeque cookout at their house. After eating, the younger folks started playing a game of softball – parents against their children. Some of us retirees were sitting on blue canvas folding chairs watching the game. We were having a pleasant conversation and somehow the subject of church came up. I asked, "Harvey, have you ever been to church in your life?"

Harvey hesitated. Then with a bitter smile he told us about his childhood some sixty years ago. He was one of seven children. His father worked at a cotton mill, and they rented a mill house owned by the company. Harvey's father struggled to provide food and to pay the medical bills of a sister who had asthma. They could not afford medical insurance. The children were entitled to free lunches at school. The backyard was turned into a garden, and the children helped their mother grow food. Sometimes, the company store refused to sell them food on credit because they had unpaid bills. Little money was left for clothing. Clothing was bought from a Goodwill Store or the Salvation Army. Old clothing was handed down from child to child.

When Harvey was about ten years old, his neighbors invited him to ride to church with them. Harvey enjoyed Sunday School. The songs were new to him; he enjoyed singing them. He was fascinated with the Bible story his teacher told. He felt goose-bumps when his teacher read from the Bible; it was the first time he had ever heard someone read the Bible. After Sunday School was over, his teacher asked him to stay, and then quietly told him, "Young man, please don't come again dressed as you are today. You should bathe before coming to church. You should wear your best clothes and shoes when you come to God's house."

Little ten-year-old Harvey looked at his torn, ragged, unwashed, unpatched overalls. His mother had not told him to take a bath, so he had not taken a bath before going to church. He looked down at his dirty bare feet. He answered softly, "No, ma'am, I won't ever." Little Harvey did not stay for the worship service to catch a ride back home with his neighbors. Barefoot, he walked the three miles home.

When he finished his story, my elderly friend Harvey stood up and ended our conversation with, "And I ain't never been back, and I ain't never going back."

Yes, I saw Harvey surrounded by his family and friends in our church for the first time on Wednesday evening. I looked down at him. He was dressed in his best navy blue suit. His hair had been cut, his mustache trimmed. He was an immaculately dressed old gentleman lying in his casket.

The first time Harvey came to church, he came on his own as a ten-year-old boy. The second time, the dead body of a seventy-three-year-old man was carried into church. As I looked down at Harvey, I thought of the little boy of long ago. I could almost hear him tell his Sunday School teacher, "No, ma'am, I won't ever."

There must have been other events that helped make Harvey so bitter toward church. Surely, the Sunday School teacher had good intentions, but she was insensitive to the situation of a poor child and contributed to the bitterness in his heart. She was insensitive to a child who was easily embarrassed. She did not understand that little Harvey could teach her about God's Kingdom. "He [Jesus] called a little child and had him stand among them. And He said: 'I tell you the truth, unless you change and become like little children, you will never enter the kingdom of heaven. Therefore, whoever humbles himself like this child is the greatest in the kingdom of heaven'" (Matthew 18:2-5 NIV).

The Sunday School teacher did not understand the love Jesus has for little children. "He [Jesus] took a little child and had him stand among them. Taking him in his arms, He said to them,'Whoever welcomes one of these little children in my name welcomes me.'" (Mark 9:36-37 NIV).

The Sunday School teacher did not understand the anger Jesus feels toward someone who hinders a little child from coming to him. Jesus became angry when his disciples tried to prevent parents from bringing their children to him. "People were bringing little children to Jesus to have Him touch them, but the disciples rebuked them. When Jesus saw this, He was indignant. He said to them, 'Let the little children come to me, and do not hinder them, for the kingdom of God belongs to such as these. I tell you the truth, anyone who will not receive the kingdom of God like a little child will never enter it.' And He took the children in his arms, put His hands on them and blessed them" (Mark 10:13-16 NIV).

The Sunday School teacher also did not understand that God is impartial. God values both the poor and the rich. James, the brother of Jesus, wrote about the value that God has for the poor, "My brothers, as believers in our glorious Lord Jesus Christ, don't show favoritism. Suppose a man comes into your meeting wearing a gold ring and fine clothes, and a poor man in shabby clothes also comes in. If you show special attention to the man wearing fine clothes and say, 'Here's a good seat for you,' but say to the poor man, 'You stand there' or 'Sit on the floor by my feet,' have you not discriminated among yourselves and become judges with evil thoughts? Listen, my dear brothers: Has not God chosen those who are poor in the eyes of the world to be rich in faith and to inherit the kingdom He promised those who love him? But you have insulted the poor.... If you really keep the royal law found in Scripture, 'Love your neighbor as yourself,' you are doing right. But if you show favoritism, you sin and are convicted by the law as lawbreakers" (James 2:1-9 NIV).

What if the Sunday School teacher had put her arms around the dirty, ragged little Harvey and said, "Son, I am happy to see you at church. I would love to see you here every Sunday. Do come every chance you get. I would love to teach you more about Jesus. Jesus loves you, and so do I."

I pray that I will be ever-sensitive to the tenderness of a child's heart. Whenever I see a dirty child with ragged clothes, may I see in that child a great potential for serving God and others. May I see beyond the appearance and behavior of a child to the eternal possibilities within.

SERMON RATING CODE

Seminaries prepare men and women for ministry in the church. One class taught is Homiletics, the art of preaching. A professor was giving an introduction to Homiletics to first year students. The professor introduced and explained different types of sermons, and he explained how he would grade his students.

A student asked, "How do you rate different sermons?"
The professor asked, "What do you mean?"
The student asked, "You know, like movies are rated – how do you rate sermons?"

The professor thought the student was trying to draw attention to himself with a cute joke. The professor didn't take the question seriously. That night the professor got to thinking about the question, and the next class he gave his students a code for rating sermons.

G This sermon is generally accepted by everyone – always politically correct. It makes everyone feel good. People leave believing they are entitled for God to bless them with prosperity, health, their wishes, and victory over others. The congregation leaves congratulating the pastor on a "Wonderful sermon!"

PG This sermon is for mature Christians. It makes the Bible relevant to today's issues and gives suggestions on how Christians should change. But it doesn't hold them accountable for changing. The congregation leaves with some telling the preacher, "Good sermon," and others saying, "Stepped on my toes today."

R This sermon is restricted to those who are not upset by truth. It's better to preach this sermon on Prayer Meeting Night than on Sunday morning. This sermon tells it like it is. It threatens the comfortable. The congregation leaves with most mentioning the words, "disturbing" or "controversial." Sometimes, one or two people want to talk to the pastor about the sermon; however, angry deacons may want to talk to the pastor about the sermon.

X This sermon bombshells the congregation with explosive biblical truth. It makes the listeners aware of God's high expectations and their own failures. It challenges them to take risks and obey God's commands. It challenges them to confess their sins and change the way they live.

Nathan preached a sermon like this, and King David confessed his sins. However, Jeremiah preached a sermon like this, and his listeners threw him into a well. Amos preached a sermon like this and was run out of town. Jesus preached sermons like this, and listeners crucified Him on a cross. Peter preached a sermon like this, and on one day, 3,000 people believed in Jesus and were baptized; however, Stephen preached a sermon like this and was stoned to death.

The preacher never knows if the congregation will receive the X-rated message and have their lives transformed, or if they will reject both the message and the messenger. The preacher who preaches this X-rated sermon needs to have a second income and life insurance paid in full, or he needs to have faith in the Good Shepherd's ability to care for those who feed his sheep.

SIGN OF THE END TIMES

Pastor Billy Bob Backer was pastor of Red Rock Baptist Church located on County Road 24.

Several crises hit the Red Rock community in the same year – A drought killed the crops, a tornado blew down trees, an earthquake shook the houses, a locust plague ate all the vegetables in the gardens, and then a heavy rain brought flash flooding. Many church goers were saying, "It looks like Red Rock is suffering plagues of Bible times!" Some wondered out loud, "Oh, could these be signs of the end of time?"

The day after the flash flooding, Pastor Billy Bob Backer asked Deacon Bubba Jones to help him put up a large sign in front of their country church. The sign read:

The End is Near
Turn Around
Before It's Too Late

The pastor and deacon dug two post holes, put the posts into the holes, and nailed the sign onto the posts:

The End is Near
Turn Around
Before It's Too Late

A pick-up truck sped by and a passenger leaned out the window and yelled, "Religious nuts."

The pick-up truck went out of sight over the top of the hill, and the pastor and deacon heard screeching tires and a big splash.

Deacon Bubba Jones said, "Preacher, I told you the sign should just say, 'Bridge Out!'"

SINGLE SHOT .22 RIFLE

Maynard was nine years old the year his brother Douglas was born. Maynard's father gave him a Winchester .22 caliber single-shot rifle for his tenth birthday. The gun only held a single round of ammunition and had to be reloaded after each shot. It was a youth gun with a shorter stock and shorter barrel than an adult gun.

Maynard used the gun to drill paper targets nailed to a tree, pop tin cans on top of fence posts, and ventilate paper plates tied to a string. Maynard became eleven years old, and he used his rifle to hunt squirrels for his mother to make homemade Squirrel Brunswick stew.

Maynard was fifteen, and his father gave Douglas a BB rifle for his sixth birthday. Their father promised Douglas a .22 Winchester single-shot for his tenth birthday, just like he had done for Maynard.

Maynard got part-time work and bought a 12 gauge, pump shotgun to hunt birds and rabbits, and he bought a 30-30 rifle to hunt deer. Maynard finished high school and moved to another state. Maynard abandoned his single shot .22 rifle in a closet, but took his bigger guns.

Their father had an accident that limited his ability to work; money became scarce. The father didn't have money to keep his promise to give Douglas a .22 single-shot rifle for his tenth birthday. But the father told Douglas, "Maynard left his .22 single-shot rifle here, you can shoot it."

Douglas used Maynard's gun to drill paper targets nailed to a tree, pop tin cans on top of fence posts, and ventilate paper plates tied to a string. He didn't hunt squirrels because with the hard times, his mother didn't have the energy to make homemade Squirrel Brunswick stew. By the time Douglas was twelve years old, he lost interest in target practice and never shot the .22 rifle again. The gun was abandoned to a closet in his father's house.

Maynard traveled and lived in many places while Douglas stayed in his rural community. Their father died, and Maynard returned for the funeral. After the funeral, Maynard asked Douglas, "Where did Daddy keep my .22 single-shot rifle? It was my first gun, and I wanna take it home."

Douglas answered, "You abandoned the .22 rifle. Daddy said I could have it."

Maynard left home again, never to return, and never again to speak to his brother Douglas.

Many years past. Maynard became an elderly man. Health problems forced him into hospice care. One day Maynard's wife told him, "Honey, your brother Douglas wants to visit you."

Maynard answered softly, but with resolve, "I never wanna see him again. He cheated me out of my .22 single-shot rifle, and I'll never forgive him!"

An old man with just a few days to live lay in his bed. He would face eternity and never see his brother again in this life. His mind and spirit were in anguish; his family tie with his brother was broken over a single shot, .22 rifle he had abandoned and his brother never used."

SMART DONKEY

The donkey is the smartest animal on the farm. Children must go to school to learn their vowels: a-e-i-o-u; however, the donkey knows his vowels without even going to school. You can hear the donkey saying his vowels, "AH-E-I-O-UUU!"

Jack the Donkey was out in the pasture the day Mr. Farmer dug a deep well close to the path that leads to the barn. That evening, Jack wandered to the barn to get the hay that Mr. Farmer always put out every evening. Jack fell into the deep well. Mr. Farmer didn't have a tractor to pull Jack out of the well. Mr. Farmer was afraid to go down into the deep well to put a harness under Jack. Mr. Farmer was afraid that Jack would fight to get out of the well and squeeze him against the side of the well. Then both Mr. Farmer and Jack would be down in the deep well.

Mr. Farmer said, "There's no way I can get Jack out of the well. Now, with Jack in the well, I won't be able to drink the water. I don't see any option. I'm gonna have to bury Jack in the well."

Mr. Farmer got his shovel, scooped up a shovel full of dirt, and threw the dirt into the well. When the dirt hit Jack on the back, Jack went shake-shake with his back and stomp-stomp with his feet.

Now what happened when Jack was hit with a shovel full of dirt and he went shake-shake with his back? What happened when he went stomp-stomp with his feet? *(The storyteller can invite the listeners to shake-shake and stomp-stomp with him.)*

Every time Mr. Farmer threw a shovel load of dirt into the well, Jack went shake-shake with his back, and stomp-stomp with his feet.

Mr. Farmer kept shoveling and throwing dirt into the well. And, Jack keep going shake-shake and stomp-stomp. Mr. Farmer could not bury Jack in the well, because every time he threw dirt into the well, Jack went shake-shake and stomp-stomp.

Mr. Farmer kept shoveling dirt into the well, and Jack kept going shake-shake and stomp-stomp, until the well filled up with dirt and Jack climbed out.

SNAKE FIGHT

A fisherman was walking on a dirt road to a creek and noticed two long slender black snakes, about the same size, engaged in a fierce combat. The two snakes went round and round, contracting and expanding, twisting and turning, struggling with all their strength to overcome each other. After about twenty minutes, the snakes became so tired that they could barely move.

Then the two snakes changed their mode of fighting. One black snake grabbed the end of the other's tail in its mouth and began to swallow. The other snake grabbed the first snake's tale and began to swallow. Both snakes kept on swallowing each other until the two snakes were in the shape of a hoop. The two snakes kept trying to swallow each other and the hoop shrunk in distance around but increased in thickness. Then there were two adjacent, gaping snake heads facing opposite each other with the short but incredibly thick body of the other in their mouths. The snakes eventually reached a point where they couldn't continue to swallow. When neither snake could swallow any more, they laid together in the shape of a hoop. The snakes made no effort to free themselves from the other. Their only effort was to try to devour more of the enemy. When they could swallow no more of their enemy, they lay still in the shape of a hoop until they both died.

This story reminds me of the way many politicians act. Their primary concern is to destroy members of the other party. It is also the way many polarized groups react to other groups who disagree with them. Their primary concern is to destroy the enemy group that disagrees with them. But the one whose primary concern is to destroy the enemy is also destroying himself.

S.O.B. CHURCH MEMBER

Debbie worked in different hospitals for about thirty years. She started out as an admissions clerk. She was the first person a new patient dealt with upon entering the hospital. Debbie took down the patient's personal and medical information. Debbie moved up the promotional ladder until she became Admissions Director – responsible for managing and supervising the admission's staff.

Debbie was single. Whenever a married employee needed time off, the hospital asked Debbie to fill in. Debbie loved her job; however, she didn't like being constantly called in to work on her days off. If she stayed home when on vacation, the hospital called, asking Debbie to come to work.

Debbie read in her church's bulletin that the church needed a Church Administrative Assistant. The administrative assistant's weekly duties included: answering the church's phone; preparing bulletins for worship services; adapting the pastor's sermon outline into a PowerPoint presentation; keeping the church staff and members informed about prayer requests; and serving as the senior pastor's personal secretary. Debbie applied for the job and was hired.

The senior pastor emphasized to Debbie, "It's important for church staff to know about members who are hospitalized. If someone phones the church to report a church member has been hospitalized, immediately send a short e-mail to all staff member's cell phones. Include essential information such as name, reason for hospitalization, and name of hospital.

The second day Debbie was on her job at the church, she sent the following e-mail to all staff members, "Sally Peterson – SOB – Mercy Hospital."

An hour after Debbie sent the e-mail, the senior pastor and assistant pastor stormed into Debbie's office. The senior pastor asked, "Debbie, what is wrong with you?"

Debbie answered, "Nothing is wrong. Why did you ask?"

The pastor answered, "You said Mrs. Sally Peterson is S O B."

Debbie asked, "Do you know what S O B means?"

The pastor answered, "Yes. S O B is a vulgar acronym for a disgusting person. It's a vulgar expression that should never be used by any staff person of this church!"

Debbie gave the sport's time out hand signal and said, "Time out! Do you know what S O B means as medical acronym?"

The pastor answered, "No. What does it mean?"

Debbie answered, "S O B is the medical acronym for Shortness of Breath."

STIR WHAT YOU GOT

Southern cooking may be fried chicken, fried catfish, or barbeque pork. But Southern cooking is always accompanied by tall glasses of cold, sweet tea. Waitresses at Southern restaurants give their customers a choice, “Do you want sweet or unsweet tea?” A Southern restaurant would never expect customers to sweeten their own tea.

A southern family took a vacation to the Rocky Mountains. They crossed the state line from Texas into New Mexico. The father noticed that whenever they stopped at a restaurant and he asked for sweet tea, he was told, “We don’t serve sweet tea. Sugar is on the table for you to sweeten it yourself.”

The family crossed into Colorado. The family hiked a mountain trail. That night they went to a restaurant to eat. The father was dehydrated from the dry air, high altitude, and unaccustomed exercise. The father asked the waitress, “May I have some ice cold, sweet tea.”

The waitress replied, “We don’t serve sweet tea. Sugar is on the table. Sweeten it yourself.”

The waitress brought the tea, and the father poured sugar from the sugar container into his tea. The father drank the glass of tea; he asked for another glass of tea. The father poured more sugar into the glass of tea and drank it all. Then he asked the waitress for another glass of tea. Then the father noticed that the sugar container was empty. He tried to get the busy waitress’ attention. The busy waitress finally came to his table and the father said, “The sugar container is empty. I need sugar to sweeten my tea!”

The waitress observed that the bottom fourth of his glass contained undissolved sugar. She said, “Honey, stir what you got. You don’t need more sugar, you need to stir what you got.”

THANKFUL DURING HARD TIMES

Our son, Tim, married Leslie. Four years later, their daughter Anna was born. Tim gave thanks to God that Anna was born healthy. Nine years later, twin girls, Jaclyn and Isabella, were born, and Tim and Leslie gave thanks to God that they had three healthy daughters.

Tim and Leslie live with their three daughters in Red Oak, Texas, a suburb of Dallas. Leslie was a school teacher and took all her sick days for maternity leave after the birth of the twin babies. Tim was a principal at a middle school, and since he had sick days available, he took the afternoon off work to take the twin girls to the doctor for their regular nine-month check. Tim was thankful to be the father of two healthy babies.

The doctor examined Jaclyn first and declared her a healthy baby. Then he examined Isabella. The doctor called in a nurse and said, "I need someone to hold a baby for me." The doctor told Tim that he needed to show him something with Isabella. The doctor poked Isabella some more and had Tim feel her stomach; then he called in another doctor and said, "Examine Isabella. I'm stepping out of the room so I won't influence you in any way."

The second doctor examined Isabella and left the room. The two doctors returned and told Tim, "We made an appointment for Isabella to have a sonogram."

Tim replied, "When would you like us to go?"

The doctor said "We've made an appointment for Isabella to have a sonogram tomorrow in Plano, Texas. That's the only hospital that can do the sonogram tomorrow."

The next day, Tim and Leslie drove the hour to Plano for Isabella to have the sonogram at 8 a.m. During the sonogram, they saw that Isabella had a mass in her stomach. After the exam, a lab technician told them, "You have an appointment with an oncologist at Children's Hospital in Dallas."

Tim got out his iPhone to record the time of the appointment and asked, "When?"

The technician responded, “Today, the oncologist is expecting you at 11 a.m.”

Tim and Leslie went to Children’s Hospital and were sitting in the waiting room with Isabella in Leslie’s lap. A girl, who looked to be about twelve years old, approached them and asked, “Is that your baby?”

Tim answered, “Yes.”

The girl asked, “Does she have cancer? My two-year-old brother has cancer.”

Tim and Leslie realized they were in a hospital building where if parents brought in a child, everyone assumed the child had cancer.

The oncologist met with Tim and Leslie and said such words as, “Cancer....Neuroblastoma....More tests....Surgery....Chemo....More tests to know more...Take one step at a time...It’s going to be a long hard road ahead of you...She may enter kindergarten with cancer.

Within the next few weeks, Tim and Leslie realized that the hospital would become their second home. The medical staff advised them, “Keep a bag packed with a toothbrush and a change of clothes, so anytime Isabella has a fever you can immediately bring her to the hospital.”

Tim and Leslie no longer thanked God for three healthy daughters; rather, they thanked God each day they have the blessings of being together with each of their three daughters. For eight years, Tim and Leslie faced life having a daughter with stage four cancer. Just as a magnet attracts metal, Tim and Leslie have attracted other parents who have followed them onto the long hard road of having a child with a chronic illness.

ooo

After living with stage 4 cancer for six years, a surgeon in New York City removed 99% of Isabella’s cancerous tumor. She still has a stage four cancer but the cancer is not reproducing new cancer cells at the time I’m writing this book.

TOO THANKFUL TO BE TIRED

An elderly lady drove to the University of Alabama Hospital in Birmingham. The parking garage was full, and she had to park on the fourth level deck. Then she walked the length of a football field to the elevator. She took the elevator to the second floor and had to walk the corridor for the length of another football field to enter the hospital. She was out of breath when she boarded another elevator to go to the eighth floor.

The elderly lady entered the elevator, and an elderly man using a walking stick followed her into the elevator. The man was breathing hard and leaned against the side of the elevator. The lady said, "It's a long walk from the parking garage to the hospital. You look as tired as I am."

The man answered, "It's a long-long-long walk; I've made it every day for the last 90 days."

The woman said, "You must be worn out."

The man answered. "No. I'm not worn out. Every day I make the walk means that she is still with me."

TWO BROTHERS

Many, many, many years ago, a farmer had two sons. When the boys were little, they helped their father with the farm work. Each year, the father gave the boys more farm chores to do. When the brothers became men, they continued to work for their father on his farm. The soil was rich, the animals were healthy, the father and sons worked hard, crops produced in abundance, more land was purchased, and the barn was full at the end of harvest time.

One brother courted and married a neighbor's daughter. The other brother remained single. The married brother had many sons; the single son had no children.

The father died and the two brothers remained together on the farm and worked it as one operation. They were partners. They shared the planting, cultivating and harvesting. They divided the harvest in half. Together, they built a house for the single brother. Together, they remodeled their father's old house for the married brother. Together, they tore down their father's old barn. Together, they built two barns, one for each brother.

Together, they cleared the land and planted barley, wheat, and a vineyard. Together, they prepared a pasture for the livestock – the cows, sheep and donkeys. Together, they worked the fields to remove the weeds from the crops. Together, they harvested their crops. Together, they daily checked on their animals, and, together, they fed the animals.

The soil was rich, the animals were healthy, the brothers worked hard, and crops produced in abundance. More land was purchased and the two barns were full at the end of harvest time.

One day, the single brother thought, "It is not right. It is not right for my brother and I to divide the crops in halves! He has a large family to feed, and I only have myself to feed. I will do the following: Every night, I will go to my barn, get a sack of grain, and take it to my brother's barn." That is what he did. Every night, he got a sack of grain from his barn, put it on his shoulder, and silently slipped it into his brother's barn.

About the same time the married brother thought, "It is not right. It is not right for my brother and I to divide the crops in halves. I have many children. When I am old and can't work, my children will take care of me. However, my brother has no children. When he is old, there will be no one to take care of him. He needs to save for his old age. I will do the following: Every night, I will go to my barn and get a sack of grain and take it to my brother's barn." That is what he did. Every night, he got a sack of grain from his barn, put it on his shoulder, and silently slipped it into his brother's barn.

Every morning, each brother was confused and asked himself, "How can it be? Every night I take a sack of grain to my brother's barn, and yet my stock of grain doesn't decrease?"

One dark, dark night, each brother left his house at the same time, each brother got a sack of grain from his barn at the same time, each brother put the sack on his shoulder at the same time, and each brother silently slipped toward his brother's barn. The two brothers bumped into each other halfway between the two barns. Each brother had a sack on his shoulder. That is when each brother understood why his stock of grain never decreased. Surprised, full of joy, each brother threw his sack on the ground and grabbed his brother for a long hug.

God looked down from Heaven at the two brothers hugging each other and God said, "That is holy ground, because on that place, there is great love."

ooo

This is a Jewish folktale. Jewish folklore states that it was at this very location that King Solomon built the temple for the Jews to worship God.

UNFORGIVING COST

It was high school, senior prom day. Faye was going with Joseph – a dream come true. Early afternoon, she tried on her prom outfit, so Mother would have time for any last minute alterations. Faye practiced her dance moves, and the right heel of her new blue shoes cracked and broke.

Faye sobbed, "Mommmaa! It's two hours 'til Joseph comes. What am I gonna do? I don't have shoes that match my dress!"

Mother said, "Your pair of white shoes will do fine."

Faye sobbed, "They're old and scratched. They don't match my blue dress. All the other girls got new shoes. I can't go like this. I'll call Joseph and cancel. I can't go looking like this."

Daddy sneered, "Stop your melodramatics! Learn to make do, or do without. Wear your white shoes or call Joseph and cancel."

Mother said, "Honey, you don't understand. She's seventeen and the world revolves around her. This prom is one of the most important days in her life. I'll make it to the mall, swap her shoes and be back before Joseph gets here."

Daddy argued, "Let her learn! The world doesn't revolve around her. She can't always have her way. If someone has gotta go, she's got a driver's license, let her go."

Mother replied, "Honey, calm down. Stop fussing. A seventeen year old needs time to get ready for one of the most important nights of her life."

Faye started her bath; Mother left for the mall. Two hours passed and Joseph arrived. Faye told him that she would be ready as soon as Mother returned with her shoes. Headlights turned into the driveway, but it wasn't Mother. It was the sheriff who informed them that her mother had been speeding, wrecked the car, and had died on impact.

Daddy rarely spoke to Faye after the accident. They never ate together. Daddy ate on the way home from work, and Faye heated TV dinners for herself.

One day, Faye saw her father looking at family albums and sobbing. Faye cried, “Daddy, I’m so sorry.”

Daddy replied, “You walk around looking like her and talking like her. Every time I see or hear you, I’m reminded that your melodramatics sent her to her death. I’ve not turned you out because she wouldn’t want that. She set aside money for your education. It’s yours. But when you leave for college, I never want to see you again!”

The father would not forgive his daughter, so he lost his wife and daughter on the same day. He never knew his grandchildren. He died a lonely, bitter old man.

UNFORGIVING HEART – POLICE HEADQUARTERS

Many people's hearts are similar to the computer program at police headquarters. The police station has a computer program with files on individuals and their criminal actions. You can ask, "What do you have on John Smith? What have you on Joe Blow? The policeman can open the file and give you a printout of the wrongdoings of John Smith and Joe Blow.

We're often like that. We keep files in our minds of the wrongs others have done against us. At anytime, we can recall and share the information. Sometimes, with real grace, we leave the file closed and do not talk about the cases; yet, when necessary, the file is still there so that the cases can be brought to light.

As long as we have a police file against someone in our hearts, we can't forgive them. With this computer file in our heart, we are holding a grudge against the person who has wronged us. Obeying God's will becomes possible only after the file has been deleted. We must be as firm as a rock in this matter: we will not be a police computer with files stored in our hearts that list the wrongs other people have done against us.

UNFORGIVING SISTER AT FUNERAL

My wife and I went to the funeral of a lady who was a friend and co-worker. My friendship began with her and the man she married when we were in university together. Years later, my wife and I were co-workers with the lady and her husband.

The husband asked my wife and me to join the family for a meal before the funeral service. The house was full, some eating in the kitchen, others in the dinning room, and others sitting on couches in the living room. My wife and I were sitting on a couch eating, and talking to the sister of the deceased, who sat in a chair across from us.

The husband of the deceased entered the room and asked the sister of the deceased, "Have you seen your brother?"

The sister answered, "Yes, I saw him?'

The husband asked, "Did you speak to him?"

The sister answered, "No, I didn't speak to him!"

The husband cried out, "There's no hope."

The sister said, "Everything is going to be all right."

The husband said, "No, it's not all right. My wife prayed since she was in high school that you'd start talking to your brother again. If you refuse to talk to him at your sister's funeral, there's no hope!"

The sister answered, "You don't know the whole story."

The husband said, "No, I don't know the story. You've never told anyone why, when you were in high school, you got mad at your brother and stopped talking to him. In fact, your father ordered you to tell him what was wrong or he would take away your car keys, you took your punishment rather than tell. Nobody knows why you won't talk to him!"

The sister put her food on the coffee table, got up, walked out of the house, got in her car, and drove away; leaving before her sister's funeral.

UNOPENED PACKAGE

Miss Cathy was in her fifth year of teaching second grade. Miss Cathy's favorite student was Sarah Grace. Sarah's mother died the year Sarah was in kindergarten. Mr. Grace sent a note to ask Miss Cathy, "Would it be possible for Sarah Grace to stay after school an extra half an hour each day, until I get off work."

Miss Cathy answered, "It would be a joy to have Sarah Grace help me straighten up after school."

Each day, Mr. Grace came to the class room to pick up Sarah Grace. He was very shy and never said more than, "Thank you, Miss Cathy."

Christmas came, and most students gave Miss Cathy gifts. Miss Cathy could tell by the packages what was inside. Most were either books or handkerchiefs. She opened each package that contained a book, but put the long thin, still wrapped boxes with handkerchiefs inside a closet. Whenever she needed a handkerchief she went for an unopened package. Miss Cathy felt that she had more handkerchiefs than she would ever need in her entire life.

The school year ended. Summer vacation came. One summer day, Miss Cathy was digging in her flower garden and cut her finger. She needed a clean cloth to wrap around her finger. She went to the closet and grabbed a wrapped handkerchief box. She ripped off the wrapping paper, and opened the box. Instead of a handkerchief, a beautiful necklace and a note was inside. The note read, "Miss Cathy. This necklace is a token of appreciation for all you have done for Sarah Grace. Sarah loves you. I would like to know you better. Would you be willing to have dinner with Sarah and me?"

Miss Cathy realized that after Christmas, Mr. Grace never came to the classroom to pick up Sarah. He sat in his car waiting for Sarah to look out the window when it was time for her to go home.

All that time, Miss Cathy possessed a beautiful necklace and didn't even know it. All that time Miss Cathy possessed an invitation that could change her life and she didn't even know it.

SLOW WAITRESS

My wife and I lived in a motor-home full time for two years. We spent time in Alabama, Georgia, Texas, Oklahoma, Montana, Florida, and Tennessee. We were staying at the Fish Camp RV Park close to Orlando, Florida, from January through March of 2007. One of the closest restaurants to our RV park was Applebees. We drove past Applebees to go to Walmart, Home Depot, or to get on the major highways.

Applebees became our favorite place to eat out. We averaged eating there two times a week. We enjoyed the excellent food and service.

One Sunday after church, we went to Applebees. Our waitress was new to us, she had never served us before. Our waitress asked us what we wanted to drink. We ordered two glasses of water with lemon. She returned with our drinks and took our order. My wife and I always ordered one meal with a second plate so we could divide it. Even splitting a meal, we usually asked for a container to take home left overs. We ordered our favorite meal at Applebees, a meal of steak and shrimp, with a bowl of spinach. The meal included a dessert of chocolate cake with ice cream. I avoided sugar, but Doris loved that chocolate cake with ice cream. The waitress brought our order after a short delay.

Then we did not see our waitress while we were eating. Another waiter noticed that our water glasses were low and gave us refills. We finished eating, pushed our plates back, and waited for our waitress to bring my wife her chocolate cake with ice cream. Minutes went by without us seeing our waitress. When the hostess was seating another family close to us, I stopped the hostess and asked, “Can you inform our waitress that we need her service?”

The hostess said she would send our server to take care of us. At that point, I looked at my watch. Fifteen minutes passed and still our waitress didn't show up at our table. I stopped another waiter and said, "It looks like our waitress has forgotten us. We are waiting for our dessert and bill."

The waiter said, "I'll get it for you."

The waiter returned with the bill, but without the dessert. He apologized, "Since you had to wait, you'll get a ten percent discount next time." The bill had a statement that if we presented it to that branch of Applebees in the future, we would receive a 10% discount off our bill.

Finally our waitress showed up at our table. She apologized, "I was delayed because I had to help at the bar, and I had to prepare some takeouts."

We requested Doris' chocolate cake with ice cream. After a delay of about five minutes she brought the chocolate cake with ice cream.

Our bill was for $ 13.90, and I put three five dollar bills on the table. The waitress asked, "Would you like some change?"

I replied, "Yes, I tip for service. Since service was lacking, I'd like my change."

The waitress said, "Whatever." Then she took our money away. She returned with change of one dollar and ten cents and said, "My baby thanks you too, and may God have mercy on your soul."

My wife said in a whisper, "Wow, that was insulting!"

As we walked out the door, the hostess asked, "Was everything to your expectations today?"

I answered, "No, it wasn't. I complained about poor service, but I didn't expect to be insulted by a server."

The hostess asked, "Would you like to speak to the manager?"

I answered, "No. But tell him that I don't like to be insulted by a server."

As we walked to our car, my wife said, "We'll never eat there again."

That afternoon, my wife reprimanded my remarks to the waitress. She said, "The waitress didn't do her job. She gave us poor service. She didn't deserve a tip; however, you should have left her a small tip without criticizing her. You often say that we need to live and talk in such a way that when we talk about Jesus, people will want to listen. If you meet that waitress in the future, you can be certain that she would never listen to you talk about Jesus. If you were to invite her to visit a church, she would never accept an invitation from you."

WRECKED THE TRUCK

Once, there was a pastor who was loved by his church members and respected by fellow pastors. He was respected in his community as a man who lived what he preached. He was an outstanding preacher. He was praised by fellow pastors as a "preaching machine." His church was growing and was known for creative new approaches.

The pastor was a workaholic who put in long hours. He had time for any church member who wanted to visit with him. Most mornings, the pastor was at the hospital before 6:00 a.m. to visit with people going into surgery. When his days were occupied with people and church work, he did all-nighters preparing outstanding sermons. He seldom took a day off, didn't get enough sleep, got little exercise, had little family time, and didn't eat properly.

The pastor had a stroke, lost the use of his left side, and his speech became slurred. Fellow pastors visited the sick pastor. The sick pastor told them, "The Lord gave me a message and a truck to deliver the message. I was in a hurry and drove recklessly. I wrecked the truck; now I can't deliver the message."

My father was a workaholic farmer. My father worked alongside his field hands and didn't ask them to do something he wouldn't do. When it was raining, he'd go to a store at the crossroads and visit with other farmers; however, if the weather was good, he never took time off to hunt or fish like neighboring farmers. He always found work to do on the farm.

When I was 14 years old, my father went to the doctor with some health problem. The doctor expressed concern about my father's health and urged him to slow down, but it was time to harvest the hay. Two weeks later, my father spent the morning in the hay fields working with the farm hands. He came home for a quick lunch and nap. He got up from his nap to return to the hay field and dropped dead with a heart attack.

I'll never know, but I often wonder if my father had followed doctor's instructions and slowed down, maybe he would have lived longer.

WRITER IN HELL

A popular professor at a certain university was also a writer. He used the books he wrote as textbooks; however, his students were the only ones who bought his books.

The professor died and went to hell. He was put in a room that was as hot as Alabama in the dog days of August. He was in a room with embezzlers, bootleggers, and other non-violent sinners. Many years passed, the professor was demoted to a hotter part of hell, next door to a furnace. He was put into a room with a robber and a murder. Many years passed, the robber and murder were promoted to a cooler place in hell while the professor was demoted to a hot furnace in hell. He was with terrorists and perverts.

The professor asked a demon, "Would you please explain to me why my punishment has increased while that of the robber and murder has become lighter?

The demon explained, "The robber and murder stopped hurting people when they died. With time, the victims of the robber have recovered from their loses. The murderer turned a wife into a widow. With time the widow restructured her life, became a stronger woman, remarried and is no longer suffering. However, your books became popular after your death. Your books are now required textbooks at many universities and they are being translated into other languages. Your students have become mature adults who are teaching others the same things you taught them. As a result, you are doing more damage now than when you were alive."

WRONG PLANE

A small commuter jet service only had a pilot, a co-pilot, and one flight attendant on board each plane. One morning, a cabin crew arrived at their plane to prepare for takeoff. The flight attendant noticed passengers already standing in line at the departure gate.

The gate agent announced the plane was ready for boarding. Passengers exited the gate to walk on the outside pavement to the steps where they would board the plane. The flight attendant stood at the top of the steps by the entrance door to the commuter jet plane to welcome passengers on board and to receive their boarding passes.

The flight attendant checked the first boarding pass and told the passenger, “I’m sorry sir, you’re on the wrong plane. You’ll have to disembark and wait for the boarding announcement of your plane.”

The flight attendant was shocked to discover that the second, third, and forth passengers were also boarding the wrong plane. The flight attendant communicated with the boarding gate agent to discover if they had announced the boarding of the wrong plane.

Then the flight attendant discovered the truth, she and her cabin crew members were on the wrong plane.

WRONG PRIORITIES

A young man began a new business while he was studying at the university. The young man was too busy building up a new business to date and find a wife. He was a multi-millionaire and forty one years old when he finally married a lady who worked for his business. He and his wife soon had a baby girl. A maid took care of the little girl, and the girl's mother continued working, helping with her husband's business.

The father seldom saw his daughter. Most days, he left for work before his daughter woke up, and he returned home after she had gone to bed.

The daughter was in first grade when her father became sick with a terminal disease. The daughter didn't understand why her father, who seldom had been at home before, was suddenly always at home. But each day, the little girl returned home from school, and she ran into her father's room. She moved toys into her father's sick room and played with her toys.

Before, when the father had good health, he was too busy expanding his business to enjoy time with his little girl; now that he was bedridden, he looked forward to her daily visits.

One day, the company lawyer and co-workers visited the dying man. The little girl played with dolls while the men talked. During the visit the lawyer said, "After you're gone, your family will be well provided for." Several times the lawyer made the comment, "After you're gone."

The co-workers left and the little girl asked, "Daddy, are you going away?"

The father answered, "Yes, darling. I'm going away to a place where you won't be able to visit me."

The little girl asked, “Daddy, do you have a nice house and friends where you’re going?”

The father was silent for a minute. Then he turned to the wall and sobbed, “I’ve been a fool. Here, I’ve built a mansion. Here, I’ve millions of dollars in investments, but where I’m going, I’m gonna be a poor man!”

WRONG SHIP

Two tourist cruise ships were each rented for a three day trip to go to two different islands.

One ship was rented by a gambling club so gamblers could enter international waters and be free from restrictions of national and local laws. The gamblers expected a time of drinking, risque entertainment, partying, prostitution, and gambling.

The other ship was rented by a church to use as a time of spiritual retreat. Church members expected a time of fellowship, family entertainment, Bible study, gospel singing, worship, and preaching.

However, by mistake, a gambler boarded the church's ship, and a Sunday School teacher boarded the gamblers' ship.

Three days past. The two ships returned to dock. The first person off the gamblers' ship was the disgusted Sunday School teacher, and the first person off the church's ship was the disgusted gambler.

WRONG TRAILS

A pastor met with youth from his church for a question and answer session.

A teenager asked, "Why are eight of the ten commandants negatives?"

- Do not have any other gods
- Do not make for yourself an idol
- Do not misuse the name of the Lord your God
- Do not murder
- Do not commit adultery
- Do not steal
- Do not give false testimony
- Do not covet

The pastor told a short story. A hiker went with friends to a large forest. The hiker told his friends, "I need to retie my shoes. Go ahead, I'll catch up."

The hiker finished tying his shoes and looked up, but his friends were out of sight. The hiker became separated from his friends and lost his way in the thick forest. He wandered around seeking the road that would take him out of the forest. He came upon a trail and followed it until it came to a junction of several trails. The confused hiker didn't know which trail to follow. Then he saw another hiker coming his way. The other hiker reached him, and the confused hiker asked, "Sir, I'm lost. Can you tell me which trail will lead me safely to the road out of the forest?"

The other hiker answered, "I'm also lost." But he pointed with his finger and said, "I've tried that trail." He pointed to another trail and added, "And that trail, and neither leads to the road out of the forest."

The man's answer wasn't what the lost hiker wanted to hear, but it did give him orientation to know the trails that he shouldn't even try.

ZIPPER CATCHES TABLECLOTH

Wallace coached basketball in his hometown at the same school where he once was the star basketball player. Wallace never married. Nephews considered Wallace a gentle giant. Nieces considered Wallace a giant teddy bear. Several times, nieces attempted to get Uncle Wallace together with one of their single school teachers, but Wallace avoided all attempts to connect him with a woman.

One of Wallace's nieces asked her father, "Did Uncle Wallace ever date in high school?"

The father answered, "No, oh yes, he took Big Alice to the senior prom."

The niece asked, "Was Big Alice fat?"

The father answered, "No, Big Alice was tall. She was 6'5" and your Uncle Wallace was 6'11". Everyone laughed when the two clumsy giants tried to dance. Wallace took Big Allice home after the first dance."

The niece asked, "What happened to Big Alice?"

The father answered, "She played college basketball and then coached college basketball. She never married."

The year Wallace was sixty-nine years old, he had his first losing basketball season in twenty-two years. He retired at the end of the school year. The following year Wallace died. Wallace was survived by one brother, and several nephews and nieces. The nieces sorted through Wallace's things and were shocked to find an engagement ring inside a case.

One niece asked her father, "Why did Uncle Wallace have an engagement ring?"

Wallace's brother answered, "I didn't know he'd bought her a ring!"

The niece asked, "Who? What happened?"

Wallace's brother explained, "Wallace was shy and had limited experiences with girls; had no dating experience.

However, in college, a cheerleader became crazy about Wallace. The cheerleader initiated a relationship by asking Wallace to take her to different events. They became a couple who ate, studied, and went to events together.

"They'd been going together for several months when the cheerleader asked Wallace to go home with her for the Thanksgiving holidays. Said she wanted her family to meet Wallace. So Wallace went home with the cheerleader for the holidays. The girl's mother prepared a delicious Thanksgiving dinner. The girl's married sister and brother brought their families to Thanksgiving dinner and to meet Wallace.

"During dinner, Wallace noticed that his pants were unzipped. He quickly zipped up his pants. When dinner was over, Wallace stood up, only to discover that the tablecloth was caught in his zipper. Wallace stood up and the pull of the tablecloth got him off balance and Wallace fell to the floor, pulling the tablecloth. Dishes with food landed on top of him.

"Wallace ran out the house, jumped into his car, and drove back to the college dorm, leaving his suitcase and clothes at the cheerleader's house. The cheerleader called Wallace, but he refused her phone calls. She kept coming by the dorm to see Wallace, but he refused to see her. That cheerleader refused all invitations to date until Wallace graduated, left college, and went pro.

"Wallace never told me he'd bought the cheerleader an engagement ring."

www.ingramcontent.com/pod-product-compliance
Lightning Source LLC
LaVergne TN
LVHW050640100826
845148LV00011B/1929

* 9 7 8 1 6 4 3 7 0 1 7 3 8 *